JULIAN C ADAMS

TERRA NOVA

FULFILLING YOUR CALL TO REDEEM
THE EARTH AND MAKE ALL THINGS NEW

TERRA NOVA

For information, contact:

www.frequentsee.org

ISBN: 978-1-949709-93-3

First Edition: May 2020

This book is for Andy Carrie
Though absent from the body, present with the Lord

"God's plan is not to abandon this world, the world which he said was 'very good.' Rather, he intends to remake it. And when he does he will raise all his people to new bodily life to live in it. That is the promise of the Christian gospel."

N.T. Wright

Table of
Contents

"

What others are saying

"If you don't know what you don't know then there is no need to change, but once you know what you don't know then that is the day when everything changes. Julian Adams in his latest book *Terra Nova* does a masterful job of laying out the case that maybe the church has only grasped part of the story and that there is a bigger narrative to the Kingdom than what we may have realized. I pray that when you read this book you feel this invitation to be apart of the seismic shift that is happening in the body of Christ to understand and to actualize what it means for the Kingdom to come."

ERIC JOHNSON
Bethel Church, Pastor, Speaker and Author

"If you've heard Julian preach or prophesy you will know that he is passionate about calling people into their destiny and their design. This book is Julian at his best. It zooms out to provide a beautiful theological overview of God's design in creation and the destiny that has been made possible through the life, death and resurrection of Jesus for all humanity as well as for all of created order. The book then zooms back in to become a deeply practical as well as spiritual guide for how we can, as sons and daughters empowered by the Spirit, supernaturally participate in the ministry of Jesus to redeem lives, restore communities and rewire the culture. Julian is a prophetic voice I take very seriously, and I'd therefore encourage anyone to pick up a copy of this book."

PETE HUGHES
Lead Pastor King's Cross Church, London
and author of *All Things New*

"Christianity and its identity is changing in our generation. The theology is the same but it is maturing because we are gaining spiritual intelligence. Julian's book helps us to understand God's original path and relationship but goes deeply into our authority, favor, and connection to God. *Terra Nova* is a brilliantly written book that will have you pivoting in areas of your faith for your calling, your destiny, and your relationship with God and to the world around you. Julian himself is building perspective as a healthy, modern day reformer in the church. If you are looking for a good read to bring you an upgrade you found it."

SHAWN BOLZ
Author (*Translating God, Through the Eyes of Love*, and others),
TV Host (Including TBN's Translating God),
and founder of Bolz Ministries.
www.bolzministries.org

"In his work *Terra Nova*, Julian captures the theological and ideological concepts of bringing Heaven to Earth in our postmodern culture today. He teaches us that "work is an expression of worship," along with "everything we need concerning the provision and purposes of God is already here for us". These thoughts and precepts are groundbreaking to our faith if we can meditate and apply them to our lives. Out of this Heavenly thinking Julian gives us the key to his work in Terra Nova , "The real call for Christians is that we become the cultural architects of our cities, of our workplaces, and of our spheres of influence. When people walk into your space they should say, "This is a different culture, what is it?" *Terra Nova* beautifully teaches us that "The way you grow in favor in the spheres of influence that God gives you is through the currency of love." This book will change the way you view the Father and his Kingdom that he is establishing on earth."

BOB HASSON
Author of *Business of Honor,* with Danny Silk, Speaker,
CEO RMH Inc.

"Julian Adams is a recognized and anointed prophetic voice among the nations and a man I have the privilege to run with both as a friend, and fellow minister. I am always struck by two things when I spend time with this man. Number one, he is a man of more than just knowledge, but of true wisdom, born of the diligent pursuit of God's presence and truth revealed through His word. Number two, his ability to be kind, loving, and humble in the same moment is overwhelming. These things come across in the pages of his newest book *Terra Nova*, which is both timely and necessary for the body of Christ.

As you read through each chapter of this book you will be both challenged and invited into a greater revelation of God's purposes for mankind and yourself. This book strikes at the core questions that lie inside all of us: "Who am I?" and "What is my purpose?" Julian reminds us that God's original purpose in the garden has not changed on the other side of the cross. We have been empowered as sons and daughters of God to partner with Him to see "His kingdom come, His will be done on earth as it is in heaven." This is not just a book with great Godly ideas, but is a book that has been lived out in Julian's life, in his marriage to Katia, towards his children, and in his steadfast ministry to the world.

While reading his book through in one sitting, I was confronted with the thought that this book was both concise, yet had a staggering level of depth. It almost demands another two, three, or five reads in this calendar year, and then another each following year. This book builds and encourages each reader to step into a Kingdom perspective that has been seen in small parts throughout history, but must become our normal in the era to come. All creation is longing for redemption through the sons and daughters of God. This book is a calling to apprehend our place alongside our Father to see 'The kingdoms of this world, become the kingdom of our Lord and of His Christ.'"

BEN ARMSTRONG
Prophetic Ministry Director, Bethel Church, Redding California

"Julian has not just written a book, he's articulated with real beauty, the invitation extended to every follower of Jesus. *Terra Nova* helps us discover the great synergy between the story God is writing on the earth and the unique assignment that rests on every person's life. It's the kind of life that we don't just aspire to but can take hold of right now in very real, practical and creative ways. My encouragement is that you allow the pages of this book be a catalyst to the greatest adventure you could ever give your life to."

PHIL SMITH
Director, Jesus Culture, United Kingdom

"Julian's friendship as well as his prophetic ministry have profoundly impacted me. It was therefore no surprise to find *Terra Nova* to be packed full of revelatory insight and prophetic challenge. In these pages we are led through God's desire to use his children to restore his Edenic purposes for the world.

Alongside this, Julian doesn't hold back from addressing some of the defining issues of our time to which culture is crying out for answers, but which the church so often either ignores entirely or offers anaemic, polarised cop outs.

There are few things as important as those who follow Jesus each playing our own unique part in the Great Commission - this book will help you do just that, as you discover new facets of your own personal responsibility and destiny in collaborating with things of the Spirit."

PETE PORTAL
Core Team member at Tree of Life Manenberg,
Cape Town, and author of *No Neutral Ground*

"We are so thankful for the ministry of Julian Adams. He has made a profound impact on us personally and has become a trusted voice to our church. He is a dynamic, revelatory communicator who has always blown us away with his detailed accuracy in delivering prophetic words straight from Gods heart.

Terra Nova is a refreshing book that has life truly flowing from its pages. Its revelations will not only remind you of the nature of Gods heart and His kingdom but also empower you to partner with Him in bringing the culture of heaven to earth."

DANIEL & STARLA WEBSTER
Lead Pastors, City Lights Dubai

Ac

Acknowledgments

After writing a few books now, I am often overwhelmed by the vulnerability of making one's thoughts public. It usually leaves me feeling insecure and nervous, almost apologetic for my writing. It's only once I invite the community around me to read it that I realize that what I am writing about carries a deep resonance and connection to the reader. Only then do I feel excited about how these words could possibly shape the lives of many. It is with this in mind that I need to acknowledge a number of people who have made Terra Nova what it is.

Firstly, I need to thank the many heroes who have helped my thinking processes: Bill Johnson, N.T. Wright, George Eldon-Ladd, Katia Adams, Terry Virgo, and Shawn Bolz to name a few. Together, these men and women have helped me see the world and God's kingdom through a different lens.

Secondly, I need to thank the Frequentsee team. Gosh, you guys make me and Katia look good! Jeshua, you are a true friend and colleague who has been invaluable to me personally and to this ministry. Your hard work and excellence are appreciated more than you will know. The rewards of this ministry are to your account. Ben, the design and layout of this book are awesome. I love your creative process and love who you are!

I also want to thank Harvest Church in Durban, South Africa, and Bethel Church in Redding, California, for being a home for us in various times of transition. Thank you for being a safe place and a good place.

Lastly, thank you to the Adams family. Ezekiel and Evangeline, you fill my love tank so much. You are already part of changing so many people's lives, and are beginning to step into your destiny. You are all of my heart. You have all of my heart. I pray that as your Papa and Mama, our lives would draw you into love with Jesus more and more.

And of course, to my beautiful, wise, kind, and very brilliant Katia: your thoughts, insights, and theological eye have helped shape this book tremendously. Beyond what you do, I love our adventures and the fun we are having as we minister together. You have all of me. I love you.

Julian C. Adams
May 2020

In
Introduction

"There's no time to change your mind, the Son
has come and you've been left behind".

Larry Norman, "I Wish We'd All Been Ready"

My childhood was shaped by the imminent return of Jesus. This effectively meant that evangelism at any cost was the order of the day. If you were not in, you were on your way to hell, and you'd better believe that the earth was gonna burn up, too. Everything that was natural carried an inherent sense of decay and a shadow of sin. This made for scary evangelistic altar calls and a lack of desire for any other form of transformation.

In South Africa, as apartheid fell in the '90s, the manic craze of the year 2000 hit the Christian church, and many of us lived with gloomy predictions of a Y2K crash. Prophets of doom foretold the return of Christ and coming disasters. Meanwhile, in Toronto, at a church that met in an airplane hangar, God began to move and restore our understanding of sonship in what was called the "Father's Blessing" outpouring. In my lifetime (short as it has been so far), this has been the single most impactful move of the spirit. It began a recovery, not only one of sonship, but of our understanding of church and the kingdom of God coming on Earth as it is in heaven. It was in this season of outpouring that my life changed dramatically.

My understanding of Jesus changed, and I realized that through the life He lived, the death He died, and His resurrection and glorification, Jesus is actually changing the earth—not just rescuing us from coming disaster. I started to discover preachers and theologians who were convinced that God's desire was not to destroy the earth but to renew it and make all things new. People like George Eldon-Ladd, Terry Virgo, John Wimber, Bill Johnson, and N. T. Wright (the list could go on) began to radically change my worldview. I discovered a fresh, but ancient, truth our early church fathers believed. I finally realized that God is at work in redeeming the whole earth. He always has been. Not only that, but I finally realized He is not angry with the world. The Bible tells us that "In Christ, God was reconciling the world to Himself, not counting their trespasses against them, and entrusting to us the message of reconciliation."[1] When God does the math against sin and humanity, He no longer adds up our wrongdoing. Instead, the message of Christ means He is reconciling the world, the whole world, not just humanity, but every aspect of creation. Culture, the way our cities are built, the entertainment industry, our care of the earth, all of it is being brought under His gracious Lordship and glorious re-creating grace.

This book is my attempt at helping the church leave the building and become a part of God's glorious plan: redeeming the earth and making all things new. It is how I get to take a grace gift called prophecy, the ability to hear God's voice, and help others enter into it for the sake of redemption. We must have a much more glorious view of salvation than simply understanding it through the sense of a personal decision. Our salvation impacts everything, in every day!

Terra Nova—your call to redeem the earth and make all things new—is an invitation to dream and partner with heaven to do the impossible!

---

1.   2 Corinthians 5:19

01
Finding Eden

"By faith Abraham obeyed when he was called to go out to a place that he was to receive as an inheritance. And he went out, not knowing where he was going. By faith he went to live in the land of promise, as in a foreign land, living in tents with Isaac and Jacob, heirs with him of the same promise. For he was looking forward to the city that has foundations, whose designer and builder is God."

Hebrews 11:8-10

The city I grew up in is cradled by rolling wine farms on flint-like mountains. You can breathe refreshing sea breezes one moment and see mist and cloud pour down the landscape the next.

Visually, Cape Town is an invitation to worship Jesus for all that He has made. Yet, for me, it was a non-event. You see, I grew up in church. Churches in the '80s and '90s were driven by the sense of Jesus' imminent return, at which point He would take us out of this dreary world and "rapture" us away to heaven. Then all hell would be unleashed, and the earth and its rebellious inhabitants would be destroyed. Thankfully, I'd be one of those predestined to escape the coming apocalypse. All I wanted to do was get myself ready to leave. I would regularly thank God for my "fire insurance."

Then, I discovered beauty.

I discovered beauty in the many vineyards near where I lived—beauty so abundant that it dripped like dew, or clung like clumps of silver-dusted purple grapes on vines that curled around frames and trellises—some of which were surprisingly cross-like.

It shimmered from sunsets that turned the Atlantic Ocean to sheets of moving gold.

The world really was filled with His glory, inspiring in me more awe than some of my best moments in church.

As it turned out, I didn't really want to escape the world after all. I wanted to get married. I wanted to make a difference. I wanted to leave a legacy. I realized I didn't just want to get people saved but also to see something of the transformation promised in scripture:

the restoration of all things, the kingdom breaking out.

This is what beauty revealed to me: Jesus is Lord of the cosmos, and He wants to use you, and me, to make all things new.

THE ORIGINS OF EDEN

In the beginning, God created everything out of nothing more than His spoken word. Once the earth was formed and had taken shape, He, being perfect, declared that His creation was good.

He created a garden called Eden—a place of pleasure, life, and fruitfulness. Then, after creating man and woman, He placed them in the garden and gave them the authority to steward the garden and cover the earth with pleasure, life, and fruitfulness. He declared that this was also good.

Today, the word "good" is generally used to mean morally right or having acceptable qualities. For some, it means merely "okay." Not the best, but okay. In Genesis, the Hebrew word for "good" encompasses the idea of beauty, pleasure, and being agreeable to the senses. In Genesis 2, we see that trees were "pleasant to the sight and good for food." This garden was not just for function but for beauty, too.[1] God was saying that creation was not just good but that it was also beautiful; it was excellent, for God is the One who makes everything "beautiful in its time."[2]

God placed Adam and Eve in the garden and invited them to join Him, not just in managing the garden, but also in extending it. By design, the Garden of Eden was in a locality (the Hebrew term means "an enclosure"), and the rest of the world was yet to know the beauty and design of Eden. God's commission to Adam and Eve was to extend that garden and its beauty beyond its initial locality to the chaos that surrounded it.[3] Incredible things followed: Adam and Eve explored Eden and they expressed their creativity by naming and tending to the animals. They discovered, cultivated, and enjoyed the garden's culinary delights and did all that was involved in being the keepers of Eden.

The full expression of their God-image entailed taking on the untamed state of the earth in partnership with God. He intended that they, along with their offspring, spread the beauty of Eden beyond its original borders.

Unfortunately, humanity rejected paradise and chose a different path.

The story of the fall is well-known. Beauty got distorted when sin entered the garden. Those with dominion over the animals ended up surrendering to a serpent. In His grace, God expelled Adam and Eve from Eden through the garden's east side.

He never intended to leave humanity in an eternal state of separation from the loving community of the Trinity. He had a redemptive plan, which would bring about the fulfillment of His desire that humanity be restored into the unity of His triune being. But His plan of redemption involved a journey from where Adam and Eve left the garden. It took hundreds of years and passed through numerous locations and families on its way to another garden, a garden that lay before the tomb where Mary would mistake Jesus for a gardener.[4]

EAST OF EDEN

After Adam and Eve began their sojourn of separation from the beauty and pleasure of Eden by moving eastward, everything changed: their work turned to striving and heavy labor as they moved from rest-motivated work to toiling hard ground. In Genesis, moving east is symbolic of moving away from God's design and favor. Cain, too, moved east from the presence of God after he murdered his brother. The tower of Babel was established on the eastern plain of Shinar. When Lot separated from Abraham, he moved east to the city of Sodom.[5]

God responded by drawing humanity back to Himself. In His dealings with Israel, we see hints of how He would do it: "Moses and Aaron and his sons were to camp to the east of the tabernacle, toward the sunrise, in front of the tent of meeting. They were responsible for the care of the sanctuary on behalf of the Israelites."[6]

Later in the Bible, the tabernacle and the temple faced east; you'd have to walk west when entering them. In a sense, you'd have to retrace the steps of humanity's parents.

The Hebrew word for "repentance" is *teshuvah*, which also means "returning." It's most frequently associated with the Ten Days of Repentance just before the Day of Atonement. On that day, the high priest sacrificed a bull and sprinkled its blood with his finger to the east and in front of the mercy seat.[7] These, and many other details, anticipate Jesus, the High Priest, being crucified east of the temple. "That is why the Tabernacle and everything in it, which were copies of things in heaven, had to be purified by the blood of animals. But the real things in heaven had to be purified with far better sacrifices than the blood of animals."[8]

The job of the earthly counterparts was to serve as a copy and shadow of the heavenly sanctuary. That is why Moses was warned when he was about to build the tabernacle, "See that you make everything according to the pattern that was shown you on the mountain."[9] The sacrifice on Christ's cross was not a last-ditch attempt the Trinity thought up when Jesus was on His way to Jerusalem; it was heaven's homing signal from the start. To quote John Piper, the heavenly reality "cast a shadow on Mount Sinai for Moses to copy."[10]

While the tabernacle represented the pattern of heaven and God's domain, other aspects of the Old Testament also pointed to Eden and humanity's sojourn outside of the garden and unity with God. When Hebrews describes how one accesses the heavenly Jerusalem, it intimates that the Israelites' journey to the Promised Land was a picture of mankind's return to God.

As we see over and over again, to move east of Eden is to walk away from God's purposes for us. Ever since the fall, humanity has tended to move east of Eden. But God has always pursued us and drawn us back to Himself.

THE CITIES OF MAN; THE CITY OF GOD

From Adam, there was a consistent movement east until God found Abraham—a man willing to move west. God promised to make him into a great nation, and Abraham's response of belief was counted to him as righteousness. Abraham rose, and instead of going east in the same direction as those before him, he went west.

Cities are birthed out of community as families, friends, and people come together to establish a way of life based on a set of values. Each city is an expression of how humanity chooses to organize itself. The first city in the Bible was called Enoch and was founded by Cain, a man who felt inferior to his brother and, instead of caring for and serving him, murdered him. If it follows that cities are a reflection of the values of their leaders, then what Cain built was established upon the desire for power and approval. And this pattern continued after him. Genesis 11 tells how, as the people continued to move eastward, they persisted in establishing cities based on their greed for power, culminating in the man-centered Tower of Babel.

Abraham, however, longed for another city, for a community that did life differently than what had been modeled by those before him.[11] He looked for a city that demonstrated something more beautiful than what he had seen in his lifetime. His journey westward was a yearning for the joy of Eden, a garden that would go against the grain of what society had deemed right and fitting, a garden of beauty and delight that would birth a new community, a new city.

Hundreds of years later, we glimpse this city being brought into existence in a garden called Gethsemane, where the Christ's mission nears its fulfillment. The crucifixion of Jesus, which purchases salvation for the world, is encompassed by gardens—Gethsemane, where He surrenders Himself, and the garden tomb where He rises triumphantly in power and authority.

Hebrews 12 says that another brother, an older brother, entered the scene and He, being a citizen of a different type of city, revealed the heavenly city by releasing life, grace, and *shalom* on the earth. In the story of Genesis, the older brother, Cain, murdered his younger brother. In contrast, *our* older brother, Jesus, laid down His life for us—it was not taken from Him—and revealed a way of living, not by the exertion of power over others, but through the laying down of one's life in love. Where Abel's blood cried out for judgment, Jesus' blood cries out, "Grace! Grace! Grace! You're free!" which is "a better word than the blood of Abel."[12]

When Jesus cried, "It is finished!" it was an echo of Genesis when the Father ceased His work, sat down, and declared the goodness of creation. Jesus was ushering in the new creation that was to cover the earth. When His side was pierced, blood and water flowed,[13] heralding the birth of a new community: kingdom-minded people called to live in the reality of this new city, growing, spreading, and transforming everything around it.

This new humanity is birthed from Christ's side just as Eve was made from the rib taken out of Adam's side. This new humanity is called to demonstrate God's gracious rule and reign. His heart longs for communities of grace that will speak a different word, that live to join heaven in redeeming everything.

That is the beauty of the cross and what it means for us to live in this world. Jesus, our older brother, has welcomed us into His heavenly city, where love is power.[14]

In the New Testament, we see the work of re-creation start in the garden (the place where the passion of the Christ begins) and end in Revelation with a city coming down from heaven. The trajectory of scripture has always been about God moving from the garden to a city—expanding His domain to cover the earth. When Jesus describes this, He uses an all-encompassing phrase. Jesus calls it the kingdom of heaven.

A NEW EDEN

By laying down His life in love, Jesus began the greatest cultural revolution, and it is still impacting the world today. As Andy Crouch writes in his brilliant book *Culture Making: Recovering Our Creative Call*, "The resurrection is the hinge of history—still, after two thousand years, as culturally far-reaching in its effects as anything since. And it began with an act of trust, of supreme faith in the world's Creator." He goes on to say, "The second Adam's influence on culture comes through his greatest act of dependence; the fulfillment of Israel's calling to demonstrate faith in the face of the great powers that threatened its existence come in the willing submission of Jesus to a Roman cross, broken by but also breaking forever its power."[15]

At the cross, God redeemed what had been lost in the Garden of Eden. He has now put that garden—the hope of glory—inside you and me. Luke 17:21 says that God's kingdom is within us. He has made His dwelling place within us. Not only that, but God's original intent is still His intent. He wants to partner with us to extend His garden—His kingdom—over the chaos of this world so that things become beautiful and filled with the delights of God.

We have become the Eden space that God now works through in order to change the things around us. We get to extend God's garden wherever we go and in any of the places that He has given to us. The commission Adam and Eve received to extend the garden over the surrounding chaotic world is the commission you now receive.

The garden that is in you must be tended and spread around you. Our worldview, however, has to undergo real scrutiny and serious change if we are to impact any sphere of society. As we now are in Christ, our worldview has to be "facing westward," not eastward. We cannot be walking east of Eden. We need to discover the dwelling place of God once more because, like Abraham, we are sojourning.

Jesus' whole life was the demonstration of the kingdom on this earth; in Him, heaven and Earth connected. There are some radical implications for us, who, like Adam and Eve, are supposed to tend to Eden. The gardens we get to tend, however, are our families, relationships, workplaces, as well as spaces of creativity, re-creation, and influence.

The reality is that God's future kingdom, which was present in Jesus' life, is now present in us. The cross was the culmination of God's purposes from before time began, and it is because of the cross that Jesus' resurrection life is now covering the earth, redeeming every aspect of life for Him and His glory. His mission of healing the sick, lifting up the poor and the lepers, restoring dignity and honor to women and the marginalized, is the mission and call we now walk in.

The same kingdom is present in our life. We are the future of God's purposes on this earth today. This is why we cannot live with an escapist mentality anymore—God wants to redeem everything!

We have seen how difficult it is to hold on to a coherent view of God and the world. On the one hand, recognizing evil in the world drives some towards dualism—a view of God and the world with a great gulf between them. On the cross, however, there is no such dualism. God, says St. John, so loved the world: in Jesus, God and the world meet, and on the cross God takes on to himself the full force of the evil which his creatures have devised. The astonishing truth of the cross is that, faced with his creation in ruins, God does not reject it. He redeems it.[16]

The world still has an inbuilt longing for Eden. Cities that have been built on power, greed, and control are in desperate need of God's people to rise up and invade them with the love, joy, and beauty of the kingdom.

Now, instead of establishing cities east of Eden, we are sojourning west, to see His holy city—His kingdom and garden—established in all the earth.

---

1. Genesis 2:9
2. Ecclesiastes 3:11
3. Genesis 1:26-28; 2:15J
4. John 20:15
5. I owe this thought to Brian Zahnd. His book *Beauty Will Save the World* is highly thought-provoking.
6. Numbers 3:38
7. Leviticus 16:14
8. Hebrews 9:23
9. Hebrews 8:5, quoting Exodus 25:40
10. https://www.desiringgod.org/messages/our-high-priest-is-the-son-of-god-perfect-forever
11. Hebrews 11:10
12. Hebrews 12:24
13. Just like a pregnant woman when she goes into labor.
14. Hebrews 12:22
15. Andy Crouch, *Culture Making: Recovering Our Creative Calling*, p. 145, Kindle Edition.
16. Tom Wright, *Spiritual and Religious*, p. 41.

02

A New Creation

"Then He left the crowds and went into the house. And His disciples came to Him, saying, "Explain to us the parable of the weeds of the field." He answered, "The one who sows the good seed is the Son of Man. The field is the world, and the good seed is the children of the Kingdom. The weeds are the sons of the evil one, and the enemy who sowed them is the devil. The harvest is the close of the age, and the reapers are angels. Just as the weeds are gathered and burned with fire, so will it be at the close of the age. The Son of Man will send His angels, and they will gather out of His Kingdom all causes of sin and all law-breakers and throw them into the fiery furnace. In that place there will be weeping and gnashing of teeth. Then the righteous will shine like the sun in the Kingdom of their Father. He who has ears, let him hear."

Matthew 13:36-43

CHANGE THE WAY YOU THINK

When Jesus began His earthly ministry, He came with a specific message. His message was one of a kingdom, not just individual change. His gospel was one of God's kingdom coming to Earth, not just forgiveness of sin. He starts off His ministry with, "Repent, for the kingdom of heaven is at hand."[1]

Repentance is not simply feeling sorry for your sin; it literally means to "change the way you think."[2] Jesus challenged the people of His day to change the way they thought about God's kingdom. He was saying, "Change the way you think about the domain of God; it is now within arm's reach."

His message carried with it not only ideals but also the ability to fulfill and accomplish those ideals. In his book *The Presence of the Future*, George Eldon Ladd wrote, "The word which Jesus proclaimed itself brought to pass that which it proclaimed: release for captivity, recovery for the blind, freeing of the oppressed." He goes on to say, "His authority consisted in the power to accomplish what He proclaimed." Jesus was dangerous because He challenged the status quo from the moment He opened His mouth.

To understand the kingdom of God, and our role in expanding the garden, we have to go back to the beginning. This message Jesus proclaimed regarding religion, politics, culture, ethics, finances, and every other aspect of life was so revolutionary that it got Him killed. In order to understand why His message was so revolutionary, we must first understand the context into which He spoke and His dealings with the people of Israel.

GOD'S ORIGINAL INTENT

As we have already seen, the story began in a garden where heaven and Earth were in complete harmony. The Jewish understanding of heaven is that it is the literal dwelling place of God. The Garden of Eden was the first temple—the first place God and man dwelt together. It was a place of worship, work, beauty, pleasure, and harmony. It was perfect but unfinished, and it was expressed through increase.

Man's mission was to increase this expression of heaven and Earth, to extend God's presence over the planet. That is still His intent. We know the story of how man rejected God through sin. The result was expulsion from the domain of heaven on Earth, from experiencing intimacy, and from the wonder of dwelling with God.

God then set into motion His grand plan to redeem His people and the earth for His glory. We see evidence of this throughout the Old Testament. In choosing Abraham, God chose a man to extend His people over the earth. God is so full of grace, He chose to remain with His people. He gave them land and built a temple to contain the manifestation of His presence. He graciously confined Himself, first to a box called the Ark of the Covenant, and then to the building of the Temple, dwelling among His people (albeit in a limited way). The prophets called out for God to rend the heavens, to manifest Himself, to release His presence on the earth just like He did in the garden. Yet, they knew their sin blocked them from His domain.

Then, prophetic rumors began circulating about a day when Yahweh would send His Christ, the Anointed One, to restore God's domain and presence among the people. Heaven and Earth would be rejoined, but this time His glory would cover the earth like the waters do the sea. The call to increase the kingdom would be fulfilled when the Christ, the Anointed One, would come. Blind eyes would open, deaf ears would hear, the poor would be lifted up, prisoners would go free, and illegitimate control would be overthrown. The *shalom* of heaven would be released.

Shalom, as a word and a message, encapsulates a reality and hope of wholeness for the individual—and by extension, for the whole world. To simply define it as joy and peace, meaning a state of affairs where there is no dispute or war, does not begin to describe the sense of the term shalom.

> The webbing together of God, humans, and all creation in justice, fulfillment, and delight is what the Hebrew prophets call shalom. We call it peace, but it means far more than mere peace of mind or a cease-fire between enemies. In the Bible, shalom means universal flourishing, wholeness and delight—a rich state of affairs in which natural needs are satisfied and natural gifts fruitfully employed; a state of affairs that inspires joyful wonder as its Creator and Savior opens doors and welcomes the creatures in whom He delights. Shalom, in other words, is the way things ought to be.[3]

This is the peace with which the earth will be governed as Jesus, the fulfillment of Israel's prophetic longings, rules and reigns over all. And it's increasing. Everything will be as it was meant to be: Earth and heaven in deep intimacy and unity. *Shalom*.

HIS KINGDOM COME

The Jews believed that heaven is Yahweh's inaccessible dwelling place. This is what made Jesus' message so radical. He was, in fact, saying that the inaccessible, glorious domain of heaven is now reachable and open. In his book *Surprised by Hope*, N. T. Wright explains, "God's Kingdom in the preaching of Jesus refers, not to post-mortem destiny, not to our escape from this world into another one, but it is God's sovereign rule coming 'on earth as it is in heaven.'" He goes on to say that heaven "is a picture of present reality, the heavenly dimension of our present life. Heaven, in the Bible, is regularly not a future destiny, but the other, hidden dimension of our ordinary life—God's dimension if you like."

That's why the rich man in Matthew was invited to give up his earthly wealth—to be invited to the heavenly dimension of wealth![4] Jesus was asking him to get richer, not poorer. You will always reflect the kingdom you are more aware of![5]

When the heavens opened over Jesus at His baptism, it marked a new day in history where once again heaven and Earth walked in harmony in the very person of Jesus. We have the privilege of walking under that flow of favor because of Him. It's against this backdrop that we have to understand His parables. They speak of His kingdom and how it affects the world.

Let's be reminded of a few things about the nature of God's kingdom coming on the earth:

- It is the gracious rule and reign of God. (Psalm 103:19)
- It is power. (1 Corinthians 4:20)
- It is good news. (Mark 1:14-15)
- It is expressed in that which is small and grows in influence. (Matthew 13:33)
- There is tension in that it has come in the person of Jesus but will

fully come when Jesus returns. In the meantime, it is ever increasing through the life of Christ in us.

- It covers all! The kingdoms of this world will become the kingdom of our God. (Revelation 11:15)
- It is a kingdom of warfare. There is an enemy! (Mark 4:15)
- It is righteousness, peace, and joy in the Holy Spirit. (Romans 14:17)
- The kingdom is in you. (Luke 17:21)
- The kingdom is expressed through increasing shalom! (Isaiah 9:7)

SONS OF THE KINGDOM

In Matthew 13, we see Jesus tell the story of how God views His kingdom at work.[6] We understand that a man sowed good seed into his field and at night an enemy came in and sowed weeds. The wise landowner lets both the seeds and the weeds grow together and only separates them at the harvest, when it's easier to discern the difference between the two. Jesus is comparing this parable to what life is like in the kingdom.

For Jesus, the first expression of the kingdom is in relationship. The seeds in the parable are a metaphor for children. These are the sons and daughters of the kingdom. When Jesus walked the earth, He revealed both His Father and His kingdom. His whole life was oriented to declaring and demonstrating these two things. In doing so, He dealt with our sin, accomplished our reconciliation to Him, and provided our resurrection to new life.

The gospel does not just deal with sin but also restores individuals into a relationship with a kind Father. In his book *Mere Christianity*, C. S. Lewis penned the beautiful line, "The Son of God became a man to enable men to become sons of God." We were justified and placed in right standing with God, but we were also adopted by the Father into His family. God, in Christ, put on the clothing of humanity so that humanity could find their place of intimacy in trinitarian relationship. In his book *The Unseen Realm*, Michael Heiser puts it this way: "Because God's original plan included human participation, humanity could not be simply set aside. The solution was to become man and do what needed to be done in order to inaugurate the new Eden. And so he did. God himself became man in Jesus of Nazareth."[7] As sons in relationship with Him, we get to partake of who He is and live from His deep joy.

The difference between wheat and tares in the parable in Matthew 13 is the posture of sonship. Tares look the same as wheat for a long time, but it produces an empty head that stands tall and proud, whereas wheat produces a full head of reproducible seed, which causes the posture of the wheat to be bowed low with reproductive potential. Our position in the kingdom is sonship, but our stance is servanthood. We get to fully represent the Father's rule and reign on the earth. That's why we get to do miracles. It's why we get to disrupt the narrative of our day. If Jesus did it, you can do it too!

The kingdom is expressed primarily through sons and daughters who love the Father.

Jesus modeled what it means to be a Son to the Father. Every aspect of His ministry was rooted in His Sonship. This, I believe, is one of the primary outcomes of genuine apostolic ministry: it produces sons and daughters. Just as the Father sent Jesus, so too He sends us, from a place of deep relationship: a Father and Son on a mission together.

ADOPTION BY THE SPIRIT

We are sons, not slaves. If we don't get it settled that we are sons, then we will live as orphans for the rest of our lives, waiting for the command of God rather than the heart of God. The reason the Jews accused Jesus of claiming equality with God was because of His Sonship. In the Jewish mindset, at a particular time a son would be released to accurately represent and reveal his father to the world. If you received the son, you received the father. The son would receive the father's signet ring to prove that in all matters of his father's business, he was equal to his father! Jesus was demonstrating this truth with regard to His relationship with God. If you receive Jesus, you receive the Father.

This is also true of us! In his book *Knowing God*, theologian J. I. Packer says, "God adopts us out of His free love, not because our character and record shows us worthy to bear His name, but despite the fact that they show the opposite. We are not fit for a place in God's family; the idea of His loving and exalting us sinners as He loves and has exalted the Lord Jesus sound ludicrous and wild—yet that, and nothing less than that is what our adoption means."[8]

We are adopted sons and daughters of the King. To understand adoption, we must understand the role of the Holy Spirit. He is the one through whom we cry out, "Abba, Father!" At Jesus' baptism, He authenticated and revealed Jesus as the Son of God. John the Baptist witnessed to the world, "On whom you see the Spirit rest, this is He!"[9] The Holy Spirit was the signet ring designating Sonship and authority.

John the Baptist only knew that Jesus was God's Son because the

Spirit rested and remained on Him. And that's what happens for us when we become God's children. Compare this to the parable of the lost son[10]: a son leaves his father's house to live a life of sin and disregard for his father. He squanders his inheritance. He comes to his senses after living in a pig pen, and he decides it's a good idea to go home to his father's house. As he approaches his father's house, one translation says that the father ran to him, fell on him, and kissed him. He didn't even have a chance to try to explain his grand plan of repentance when the father began to throw a huge party for him! He pulled out the best and extravagantly blessed his son.

The bit I love is when it says the father ran and fell on him and kissed him. It is a picture of how the Holy Spirit is given to us. That phrase "fell on him" is the same phrase used when the Holy Spirit "fell on" believers in the book of Acts. The Holy Spirit is the kiss of the Father. For some of you, that might seem a foreign concept; for me, it's not. In my culture, when my dad sees me, he kisses me, because I am his son. No one else gets to kiss me. If some other dude tried to kiss me, I'd take him down! Only my dad gets to kiss me.

My own journey in understanding my adoption as a son has been one of increasing awareness of just how much Abba loves me. You see, growing up in "Christian culture" teaches you how to do things right without ever understanding the joy of being right with God. Ministry became a driving force for me rather than a joy and delight. I consistently felt the need to use my gifts and network connections and social media platforms to "prove my worth." These past few years, I have been learning to enjoy my Father's delight in me, simply because I am His son.

The Holy Spirit is poured out on us as the affection of the Father, to remind us of our sonship and our mission, and to invite others into this relationship with Him. He loves you with an everlasting love. It's not weak or watery. It's not transient or fickle. It's powerful and life changing. It's so powerful that it heals the sick, it cleanses the leper, and it raised Jesus from the dead! The Father wants to run toward you and kiss you with the very life of the Holy Spirit.

KINGDOM REIGN

Our story began in a garden and will end with a city coming down from heaven. The theme of gardens, fields, and land is all about God's rule and *shalom* coming to the earth. Israel was promised land as a start to God's reform and redemption of all nations. The controversy about the piece of land in Israel is only solved through an understanding of the kingdom. While I believe there are some specific promises for Israel as God's covenant people, I believe that God intended that through this people, and now through Jesus, who is the fulfillment of all of Israel's promises, the whole earth would become a garden, a dwelling place for His presence.

Notice that the field in the parable in Matthew 13 is owned by a farmer who represents God. The field is the world and it belongs to God, not the devil. This world is meant to come under the rulership and reign of heaven. Every aspect of society is to be covered! Psalm 24:1 says, "The earth is the Lord's and the fullness thereof." And Isaiah reminds us that "The mountain of the house of the Lord shall be established as the highest of the mountains."[11] Mountains of culture and influence, such as business, government, religion, family, education, media, arts, and entertainment, will bow low to the ever-increasing reign of God's rule. Everything will be covered with the glory of the Lord!

It was because of an outpouring of the Spirit and kingdom activity that the church was formed—with the purpose of expanding the kingdom and heaven's culture. This is the role of true apostleship. The word "apostle" was taken out of a Roman cultural setting. Apostles were sent ahead to "culturize" a new territory. They pioneered, and those who followed after them were governors who created structures to further the advance of their government. Jesus calls us to extend the kingdom, to be ambassadors to the world around us. When we recognize what He is doing in our world, we can build around it to increase kingdom activity. We must learn to take responsibility for our place of influence!

The kingdom, however, exists in tension. There's an enemy who works to thwart God's plans. In our expectation of experiencing more of God's kingdom, it's important to note that there will be defeats. Although our ultimate victory is secure, the enemy will do all he can to get us to agree with his will rather than the Father's.

The tension of the already-and-not-yet is found in the kingdom's ever-increasing nature.[12] My understanding of the sovereignty of God is that He expresses it through partnering with us to establish His purposes. The Bible is clear that we have a part to play in spiritual warfare.

The greatest act of spiritual warfare happened on a hill called Golgotha, where the enemy was stripped bare of all his authority over us.[13] Many of us misunderstand the role of the enemy in the world today. We think that the enemy has authority in this world. Matthew 28:18 says that Jesus has all authority, and Colossians 2:15 says that the enemy was stripped of his authority. It is essential to understand the difference between authority and power, because, while the enemy has been stripped of authority, he still has power.

Authority is the delegated ability to act, while power is merely the ability to function. The enemy can work, but he has no delegated authority to do so. This changes, of course, when, like Adam and Eve, we agree with him. When we agree with him, we give him permission to accomplish his purposes in our life. One of the ways we legitimize his approach is by agreeing with his perspective of us, enabling him to work his evil plans out in our lives. In Christ, however, we have authority to challenge where the enemy has been at work.

Golgotha means "place of the skull": the most significant spiritual battle we will face is not external attack but inside our skulls where the enemy is trying to get us to agree with him. We must renew our mind around who we are as God's sons and daughters if we're to enjoy all that the kingdom offers. We must repent (change the way we think) to see the kingdom! When we do, we get to see the unseen realm work for us.

As N. T. Wright says in his book *How God Became King: The Forgotten Story of the Gospels*, "New creation itself has begun, they are saying, and will be completed. Jesus is ruling over that new creation and making it happen through the witness of his church. 'The ruler of this world' has been overthrown; the powers of the world have been led behind Jesus's triumphal procession as a beaten, bedraggled rabble. And that is how God is becoming king on earth as in heaven. That is the truth the gospels are eager to tell us."

1. Matthew 3:2

2. Strong's Greek Lexicon G3340

3. Cornelius Plantinga, *Not the Way It's Supposed to Be: A Breviary of Sin* (source: Wikipedia).

4. Matthew 19:16-30

5. Credit: Bill Johnson

6. Matthew 13:24-30,36-43

7. Micheal S. Heiser, *The Unseen Realm: Recovering the Supernatural Worldview of the Bible*, n.p.

8. J. I. Packer, *Knowing God* (Hodder and Stoughton, 1988), p. 241.

9. John 1:33 (paraphrase)

10. Luke 15:11-32

11. Isaiah 2:2

12. "Of the increase of his government and of peace there will be no end" (Isaiah 9:7).

13. Colossians 2:15

03

Kingdom Design

"God is about redeeming the earth, and the only way that He is going to do it is through you and me."

Our understanding of Eden and the kingdom must shape our worldview and help us move westward. As we understand our role and God's kingdom within us, we cannot help but think differently about our lives and time on this planet. We must surely understand that how we live will look very different from how the world lives. It means we will go against the grain.

Every garden needs to be well-watered to flourish. God has called us to be a people who live in the extravagant overflow of His love and grace, for these are the rivers to our personal gardens of Eden. If we live in His flow, His garden will easily be extended to everyone who comes into contact with us. To help us do this, I would like to look at five kingdom truths.

1. EVERYTHING IS SPIRITUAL

In the Garden of Eden, everything was holy. Nothing was secular. Nothing was separate from God, for Eden was the dwelling place of God. It has always been God's desire for heaven and Earth to be together, not separate. The Garden of Eden can be seen as a prototype for the temple. Aside from how the Garden of Eden and the temple have very similar layouts and entrance points, the temple is, in Jewish understanding, the place where God meets man and where heaven meets Earth. Eden was the very first temple.

Later, God created a temple in the midst of His people so that they would be a light unto the nations. Israel, however, did not fulfill that calling. Consequently, God came in the clothing of humanity—Emmanuel (God with us)—and, in the person of Jesus, He demonstrated what it meant to be a walking temple.

A beautiful scene unfolded in John 7 when Jesus cried to the people at the Feast of Tabernacles, "If anyone thirsts, let him come to Me and drink . . . 'Out of his heart will flow rivers of living water.'"[1] Jesus was alluding to the river described in Ezekiel 47, a scripture used in ceremony during the Feast of Tabernacles. The Jews were looking to the day when God's river would flow from the temple. Jesus was saying, "This temple, built by man's hands, is no longer valid. I am the true temple. I am now the place where heaven meets Earth. I am the expression of Eden—pleasure, delight, and beauty—on the earth." His call to "come to Me and drink" is a beautiful picture of Ezekiel's river that flows from the throne (not *to* the throne) and covers the earth with life. Fruitfulness manifests wherever that river goes.

Jesus then ushered in a revolutionary shift as He said, "If you come to Me and drink, out of your heart will flow rivers of living water." He was saying to them, "Not only do you need to drink from Me as the true temple where heaven and Earth meet, but when you do, you'll also become a temple where heaven and Earth meet and rivers of living water flow—such that, wherever you go, life breaks out."

God's intention is that the river, flowing from the throne, will bless all of creation.[2] As you are the temple from which the river flows, creation is blessed through you. Everything is to come under the blessing of heaven. No place or person is irredeemable. Every single area of humanity must and will come under the gracious rule of Jesus, and all things will be made new! There has never been, nor will there ever be, a divide between the sacred and the secular. It is written, "Whether you eat or drink, or whatever you do, do all to the glory of God."[3] Everything is holy, and we can demonstrate God's divine purposes in everything.

One of the significant errors that some in the church have believed is that there is a separation between the spiritual and the physical. The result is that we give ourselves to that which is tangible around us while neglecting that which we are just as connected to: the unseen reality of heaven. There is no separation between the realm of the invisible spirit world and this physical world. For us to shift out of this false thinking, we need to grasp that out of our hearts flow rivers of living water, just as Jesus said. This will impact how we create, work, and live. The reality we are most aware of is the reality we will most reflect.

Pete and Sarah Portal are friends of mine who are well-educated white people living in one of South Africa's most violent townships. Manenberg, a township on Cape Town's Cape Flats, has been the victim of systemic and intentional oppression, both during the apartheid era and to the present day—the legacy of a nation not yet come into her own. Drugs, violent crime, and gangsterism form the way of life there. Most white people are afraid to visit Manenberg, let alone live there.

That place would be hopeless except for the fact that the kingdom is breaking out there. Pete and Sarah have gathered some of the most broken people, invited them into their family, and discipled them. Their life prompted a BBC film producer to also move into the neighborhood and establish a business that equips and trains ex-drug addicts and gangsters to edit and produce movies. They have started other businesses that empower people in the community to make a real difference in their families, neighborhoods, and world.

Although this is a small work, its impact is already being felt in Cape Town. Manenberg is starting to look more beautiful because of these lives laid down.

Grasping that everything is holy is the basis for accessing God's voice in every context and seeing the prophetic operate wherever we go. You do not have to be a prophet to hear God's voice. You just need to be a son. Essential to seeing a dynamic expression of God's voice pervading our lives is to understand that nothing is separate from God apart from sin, and He dealt with that at the cross. God is not sin-conscious. He is relationship-conscious. He dealt with sin so that you and I can enter into the joy of trinitarian intimacy. It is vital to grasp that everything is holy: your workplace, your family life, your recreation, and your creative expression are all sacred to the Lord, set apart for Him.

2. WE ARE IMAGE-BEARERS

Given our technological age, we're all familiar with icons on mobile phones and tablets—little pictures that represent something bigger. When opened by touch, they expose us to much more.

There's a sense of this in Genesis 1:26, when God created Adam and Eve—and therefore all of humanity—in His image. "Then God said, 'Let us make man in our image, after our likeness.'" Each of us is a version or a picture of God. While we were once fallen short of God's glory,[4] through Christ we have come into relationship with Him and are now reflectors of His glory.[5] As image-bearers, we're icons that reveal God to the world. We carry His presence in the world, and our mandate is to demonstrate who He is.

The reality of being in God's image can be described through the analogy of an angled mirror in which one sees two things at once. We are meant to reveal God to the world as humans, and as humans, to reflect our praise and worship back to Him. It's a two-way image. In 1 Peter 2:9, believers are called to be a royal priesthood. In other words, we are to reveal and combine the roles of royalty and service. Our royalty represents God's governance and gracious rule in redeeming the world, and our priestly service is to be a fully and unreservedly worshipful people in devotion to the King of all kings.

A few months ago, I found myself in a high-rise building, looking out over the city of Singapore. I felt overwhelmed and intimidated by the opulence and wealth of that office. As part of my personal prophetic call, I prophesy over business and thought leaders, helping shape their destiny. I was in the presence of a wealthy businessman who worked for a well-known multinational company. I remember thinking, *I need to get detailed and accurate insight in order to lead him to Christ.*

Everything about the room felt sterile and fake, so trying to hear from God in this context seemed almost out of place. Yet, I felt the Holy Spirit ever so gently say to me, "I want this man's heart, not his head; don't impress him with words, but reveal My kindness to him." I had the privilege of prophesying over this unchurched man, and what struck me was that, ahead of knowing about his destiny and getting accurate details of his life, all he wanted to know was that he was loved. The wealthy and influential, the poor and the sick, all have the same desire: to know that they're known by a loving God.

We are image-bearers. We are icons: a people who will open others up to encounter God. Our mandate is to reveal Him in everything we do through demonstrations of love; for the primary (and most potent) revelation of God is that He is love. As Christians, our announcement to the world is not that we are right, but that He is love. It shifts everything when you live like this.

3. WE ARE PARTNERS WITH GOD

"God blessed them, and God said to them, 'Be fruitful and multiply, and fill the earth.'"[6] God desired the culture of His garden—the place of incredible fruitfulness, established on a deep relationship with a loving Father—to be extended all over the earth.

Adam and Eve were to be fruitful, but it was not just about making babies; it was and is about filling the earth with His image. We are called not only to fruitfulness regarding offspring but also with regard to shaping cities, towns, and villages around His love and goodness. We are called to re-culture the earth with God's nature and character—to be cultural architects in our cities. Wherever we are, you and I get to influence geographies so that they're established and designed after heaven, becoming images that draw everyone into God's purposes. Our worldview must express who He is.

God could easily have filled the earth with Himself, but He chose to partner with us to accomplish this. The Hebrews understood that families establish the culture in a city, and, as an extension of being His image-bearers, we get to establish His culture.

God has called us to multiply what is right and beautiful on the earth. He has invited us to experience and spread His creativity—to partner with Him in making all things beautiful. This is why we are all creative and why we inherently appreciate beauty. To delight in beauty is to know the pleasure of God. To multiply beauty is to step into our true identity as we partner with Him.

The sovereign God of the universe chooses to restrain Himself to partner with us so that, through a body of believers, His purposes are steadily revealed. Do you realize the incredible trust that the Father has in you? He is inviting you to join Him in His mission. God can save the world in an instant, but He is more interested in your relationship with Him and the journey that He is taking you on to establish His love as the predominant culture in your sphere of influence.

God puts us together in the context of relationship because it is His primary way of being with us. Genesis 3:8 tells us that God visited with Adam and Eve in the cool of the evening. What's beautiful about this expression is that the word for "cool" is the word Ruach, from which we get the breath of God and Spirit of God. God, in His triune being, invites us into a relationship with Him by His Spirit. It is our life in the Holy Spirit that produces fruitfulness in relationships and in every area of our life. It is by the Holy Spirit that we're invited to discover things that cannot be known by the natural mind alone:

> For who knows a person's thoughts except the spirit of that person, which is in him? So also no one comprehends the thoughts of God except the Spirit of God. Now we have received not the spirit of the world, but the Spirit who is from God, that we might understand the things freely given us by God.[7]

We get to search the unsearchable riches of God's mind. We get to engage with His intellect. We get to join with His creativity. We get to participate with all that He is as He establishes us in Him so that we may become cultural architects for the King in the places of influence He has given to us.

My friends and heroes Titch and Joan Smith have understood this and worked it out in a profound way. Titch is a successful business-man in the city of Durban, which has one of the highest statistics of HIV-infected and affected people, and, as a result, a high number of orphans. This is now endemic in Southern Africa.

Titch is a well-known cricketer, and after suffering a breakdown, he came to God with nothing. God used Titch's life experience and re-deemed and transformed it. The power of a yes to God can change everything. Titch was baptized with an overwhelming sense of love. He was gripped by the words of apostle James: "Religion that is pure and undefiled before God the Father is this: to visit orphans and wid-ows in their affliction, and to keep oneself unstained from the world."[8]

What Titch has done since then is nothing short of revolutionary. It has not been without challenge. God took a man who had an addictive personality, and a broken marriage, and made him a world-chang-er. Stepping out consistently and using the influence that he has in sports, business, and government, he has established Liv Village—a community where hundreds of orphans have found a home. This is not an orphanage. It's a family. He has taken the marginalized and forgotten of society and not just met their basic needs but also "re-culturized" the fundamental fabric of society in that region by reestablishing the family through a demonstration of kingdom love.

Liv Village is not a commune, either. The presence of the Village in one of the poorest areas of Kwa-Zulu Natal has meant that jobs, cre-ativity, education, and a measure of stability have been provided where previously there were none.

And the place looks beautiful. The joy of finding beauty in the context of poverty is humbling. What's more amazing for me is that children are being fed, educated, and raised in the context of genuine love. This changes the prospects for hundreds of lives, setting them up for success, and leaving a legacy. Titch and Joan have partnered with God to literally change a nation.

4. WORK IS WORSHIP

"The Lord God took the man and put him in the Garden of Eden to till it and keep it."[9] This point might not be exciting for everyone, and some may want to stone me, but work is worship. In the Garden of Eden, work was not toiling. Work was not something you had to do to get paid. Work was an expression of worship.

There are two words used to describe our posture of work: to "till" is the word *abad*, and to "keep" is the word *shamar*. Both words are also used in reference to worship and to keeping God's Law (see Psalm 2:11 and 2 Kings 23:3). We work in a garden; we worship in a temple. In the first temple of Eden, we learned that work is worship. Work is not punishment. It is God's idea. Even God works! There was work to be done in beautiful Eden, and when the kingdom comes fully and makes everything new, there will still be work to be done.

Sadly, many Christians despise their workplace because they think the real activity of the kingdom happens on a Sunday morning. "I need to get to the prayer meeting instead of going to play golf, because a prayer meeting is more important than my influence on the golf course with people who don't know Jesus yet." We have to shift the way we think because life is not lived only on a Sunday morning. God's intention in the Garden of Eden was not only to have a single holy day, but also that all of life would be holy.

While I believe the church is the key to extending the kingdom, we sometimes think that the aim is to get more people into a building rather than sending more people out. True sons are sown into the world alongside those who have intentionally been sent to release demonic influence—not sheltered away from them!

In this season, we as a church have to move from an inward-looking expression of the gospel to a kingdom-looking expression. That means we don't just want to get people saved, knowing their sins are forgiven; no, we want them to be carriers, ambassadors, of the Father's kingdom.

If we are to impact the world, we have to move away from an expression of life that values gatherings and church meetings above His kingdom of love expressed wherever we go. I love the church. I am on church leadership, and I serve in the local church because I believe that the church is the most beautiful thing on planet Earth. But she is not here to gather to herself. The church is meant to leave the building and establish culture wherever she goes. This is her work. This is her worship; for everything she does unto the Lord is worship.

5. PROVISION IS ALREADY YOURS

God said, "See, I have given you every plant yielding seed that is upon the face of all the earth, and every tree with seed in its fruit; you shall have them for food. And to every beast of the earth, and to every bird of the air, and to everything that creeps on the earth, everything that has the breath of life, I have given every green plant for food." And it was so.[10]

The Lord God planted a garden in Eden, in the east; and there He put the man whom He had formed.[11]

What we learn from Eden is that provision is already ours. In the Garden of Eden, everything Adam and Eve needed in order to multiply, thrive, and be who they were called to be was already manifest in the form of seed-bearing fruit. To see the pressure of life taken off us, we must understand that everything we need concerning the provision and purposes of God is already here.

One of my mentors, Simon Pettit, left sunny Sussex in England and planted an influential church in South Africa. He pioneered an incredible ministry among the poor in Cape Town, and made this compelling statement: "The call of God creates what it demands." Your personal destiny—your call—has within it everything that is needed for it to be fulfilled.

The blessing of God does not come because of our hard work. His grace is already present in what He has provided us.

The Garden of Eden was full of life, full of seed-bearing fruit, so Adam and Eve did not have to work *for* something. Instead, they worked from a place of rest, stewarding what God had given them.

Importantly, God's commission was given after He, Himself, had rested. This reveals that our work was always supposed to come from a place of rest. God wants to bless the *rest* of our life, not the toil of our life. The sweat on the brow began only after Adam and Eve fell. Eden was initiated into action from a place of rest. Only after God and man rested did work begin. Rest should be the starting place of work.

The same principle applies to provision. You cannot earn what you already have. We are not to try to make our way through life, but rather steward what's already there. God's design in the kingdom is not to work *for* provision, but to work *from* provision, because everything you need is already available. How you steward what you have been given determines what increase you will see. This eliminates the need for power or competition. In an Edenic worldview, you do not have to outdo, outperform, or step on anyone to get ahead. God has provided more than enough for everyone to enjoy. When this is your worldview, rest is your portion.

The result of living in a fallen world is that we've built our lives according to a pattern consistent with Cain's pattern. Right at the heart of Cain's sinful act of murder was a need to outperform, to have the better offering, and to win at whatever cost. Nevertheless, we're free to understand the goodness of God in the life of Jesus because He laid down the need to use power and force to establish His kingdom. His gracious act of laying down His perfect life is now given to us as a gift.

It's this grace that sparked a change of mind in the early Reformers. Yet, I wonder if those Reformers understood justification (that our sin has been paid for) while missing the beauty of adoption. The Reformation resulted in mass psychological indebtedness to God as the judge who forgave us. Consequently, we inherited a skewed view that Jesus is approachable because He saved us from an angry God. It's good-cop/bad-cop theology based on, and reproducing, a sense of indebtedness or the need to repay a God whom we now owe. And we *do*. We owe *everything* to Him—but not in the sense that we normally think.

You see, justification is not the aim of our salvation. Adoption is. Our Father worked through Christ to free us from ourselves so that we could enjoy an inheritance with His begotten Son, Jesus. You don't work for an inheritance. Parents do that, so their children receive and enjoy the inheritance. It is my observation that the Reformers grasped justification (and what it means for kingdom theology) but then worked really hard to keep it. J. I. Packer unpacks this idea in his book *Knowing God*:

> You sum up the whole of New Testament religion if you describe it as the knowledge of God as one's Holy Father. If you want to judge how well a person understands Christianity, find out how much he makes of the thought of being God's child, and having God as his Father. If this is not the thought that prompts and controls his worship and prayers and his whole outlook on life, it means that he does not understand Christianity very well at all. For everything that Christ taught, everything that makes the New Testament new, and better than the Old, everything that is distinctively Christian as opposed to merely Jewish, is summed up in the knowledge of the Fatherhood of God. "Father" is the Christian name for God. Our understanding of Christianity cannot be better than our grasp of adoption.[12]

It's worth commenting that because the Reformers helpfully deconstructed the divide between sacred and secular, work became a vocational response to God's grace. As Martin Luther insightfully wrote in *The Babylonian Captivity of the Church*:

> Therefore I advise no one to enter any religious order or priesthood ... unless he is forearmed with this knowledge and understands that the works of monks and priests, however holy and arduous they may be, do not differ one whit in the sight of God from the works of the rustic labourer in the field or the woman

going about her household tasks, but that all works are measured before God by faith alone.[13]

The contrary paradigm, that is, an emphasis on justification unbalanced by an emphasis on adoption, produced a hard work ethic (the "Protestant work ethic"), which was often driven by an attempt to show one's gratefulness and indebtedness to God, and rebuff accusations that the teaching of "grace alone" produced laziness.

Material increase was seen as a sign that God was blessing the Protestant work ethic and the ideas prior to it. This paved the way for a works-based response to grace, elevating riches and material gain as a sign of God's approval. It was as though the Adam in people embraced the sweaty-brow paradigm with a vengeance. I wonder how much of that thinking has shaped modern-day capitalism? Our true aim shouldn't be a self-effort work ethic, but Spirit-empowered stewardship.

Metanoia (repentance), or a powerful shift in thinking, must take place if we are to understand and operate in kingdom economics. Capitalism says, "You need to work really hard and step on whoever you need to step on in order to get what you need. You must be the most competitive to secure the deal!" Sadly, many Christians in business are often more ruthless than other business people because of this belief. This happens only when we have taken God's place as provider.

But the kingdom of God is not capitalistic in nature, for it says, "There is more than enough for everyone, so competition is not your drive. You are to be driven by stewardship, integrity, and wisdom." You don't have to be the one who fights to get the best deal. You don't have to be the one who destroys someone else to get ahead.

A good friend of mine taught me this lesson in a powerful way. Clint is a creative entrepreneur with a unique ability to network relationally, putting the right people in a room together. He's helped broker significant breakthroughs for companies, once securing a multimillion dollar cryptocurrency deal in the financial sector. This deal was his ticket and could have benefitted him in amazing ways. But through a series of unethical maneuvers, Clint was unfairly dismissed.

He had every right and legal advantage to take this particular company to court, but God spoke to him. In a moment of waiting on God, he felt God tell him not to go to court but to "abide and glide." Clint is one of my best friends and one of the hardest working people I know. But he did just what God said; he worshiped and enjoyed God. Without needing to destroy the name of the company he formed, and by walking in integrity, he saw God bless him within the next few months in unusual ways. This took him into a new season of favor and material blessing—a season whose harvest outshone what he invested in the previous deal. Rest is the operating system of heaven.

In the Garden of Eden, Adam and Eve needed nothing. Before the fall, they were naked; after the fall, they were naked. There was no external change to their surroundings and to their circumstances, yet after they sinned, they needed a covering. Poverty entered because of sin. Sin sets us up as providers rather than stewards who trust in the goodness of God. The spirit of poverty has nothing to do with how much you have or do not have. I believe poverty is the systemic recurrence of humanity's predisposition to rely on our own efforts to provide, rather than recognizing God as the one who provides for us. It's not that those who live in abject poverty are living in sin; rather, the sin of self-provision has become the default in most societies. The result is widespread poverty. When your central need is to provide for yourself, it produces striving, competition, and jealousy. This thinking has been duplicated from one generation to the next, and we need it to stop. The choices we make today have a massive impact, and when we start to model a different way of living by making financial choices that reflect heaven, we disrupt the systems that have kept people in poverty for years.

It's precisely why there was no lack among the 5,000-plus community members of the Jerusalem church in Acts. The understanding that God has availed provision produces rest. When you live with the mentality that God is your provider and you are the steward, then what you faithfully steward will consistently multiply. This is dynamic kingdom economics.

Understanding and living by this dynamic—God wanting to bless the *rest* of your life—is most often tested in your generosity. I have heard many people say, "One day, when I get my millions, I'm going to bless the church; just watch and see." "When I make my millions, I promise you, Julian, I'm going to write a check to your ministry." If I had a few hundred dollars every time that was said to me, I would be very wealthy. The truth is, if you are not generous with what you do have, you will never be generous with your increase. The degree to which you are generous is the degree to which you understand this principle of stewarding God's provision. God is looking for outrageous generosity from His people because it is the nature of His kingdom to be generous.

When you begin to look at the world, your surroundings, your family, your space of influence, the creative areas that you have, you start to realize something very powerful: God is about redeeming the earth, and the only way that He is going to do it is through you and me. We can have protracted meetings, revival meetings, and healing services, but what is actually going to change the world are the people who have an Eden-consciousness and who live demonstrating the reality of heaven and kingdom design.

1. John 7:37-38
2. Ezekiel 47
3. 1 Corinthians 10:31
4. Romans 3:23
5. 2 Corinthians 3:18
6. Genesis 1:28
7. 2 Corinthians 2:11-12
8. James 1:27
9. Genesis 2:15
10. Genesis 1:29-30
11. Genesis 2:8
12. J. I. Packer, *Knowing God*, p. 201.
13. Martin Luther, *The Babylonian Captivity of the Church*, p. 1520.

04

Your Creative Inheritance

"Let Us make man in Our image."

Genesis 1:26

We are living in a world of dramatic change. I love the fact that God is unlocking all sorts of technology and that development is accelerating—it seems that as soon as something new is released, something better comes out. This development feeds other forms of creativity, but it can also breed a competitive atmosphere where we try to always be one step ahead of each other.

Another option to keeping up with this constant development is just to imitate what has already been created. When this is true of the church, however, the results are disappointing. We call God the Creator and believe He designed us in His image. This means that we, too, are creators. The temptation to imitate exists only because we believe our lives are dull and unimportant, so we mimic others rather than truly express ourselves.

This is the tension of our world. One of the biggest lies that this generation has been sold is that your individual story does not matter. The other is that every single opinion deserves public recognition. Somewhere between the self-importance accentuated by social platforms and the false-humility and self-emptying emphasized by the church is the truth: the importance of being ourselves for the sake of glorifying Jesus.

A key to being the creatives God has designed us to be is being a people who are genuine and authentic. It's through such people that God will establish His purposes.

How do we move from copying to being authentic? How do we move from imitating to genuinely creating? How do we release our true selves? Our inherent creativity and purpose flow from our relationship with God—our understanding of His love and of our own identity as sons and daughters of the King. When we know who we are, and the impact we can have on this world, we begin to express the creative nature of our Creator.

UNDERSTANDING YOUR WORTH

The Bible is full of stories of individuals who seemed insignificant in their day. In retrospect, we see clearly how significant their lives really were. A stuttering shepherd, Moses, was chosen by God to lead millions of Jews out of Egypt to the Promised Land. God used a seemingly insignificant woman, Esther, to save a whole nation and become its queen. Daniel, held in captivity under an oppressive regime and unable to freely practice his religion, became an advisor to the highest level of office. Joseph was left for dead and sold into slavery by his family, but God lifted him up to such a place of significant influence that he became "a father to Pharaoh."[1]

God chooses individuals to shape the course of history. Your story—no matter how big, no matter how small, no matter how dramatic or insignificant it might seem—has huge significance in the kingdom.

Billy Graham was a highly respected man of God who had significant influence, but I often wonder if the man who led him to the Lord wasn't perhaps the real influencer in his story. We often forget who is behind the scenes. Yet this man's life, in terms of greatness, is going to be rewarded all of the fruits that Billy Graham saw in his lifetime and beyond.

We never know how greatly our lives impact people. I know for me, the catalyst to understanding this impact was a Scottish woman called Fay Macbeth. Aunty Fay, as I affectionately knew her, became a close family friend. Having grown up in Glasgow before moving to South Africa, she was widowed, with a family of five to care for. Fay was slightly eccentric, a lover of the Holy Spirit, and a powerful evangelist. In her life, she impacted thousands by obediently leading people to Jesus, people who then went on to have significant ministries.

Mine was one of the lives she impacted. I clearly remember, as a child, walking into the lounge at home where she was talking with my mom; in mid-flow, she told me of a dream where I was prophesying the secrets of people's hearts. In that electric moment, I was set apart for the ministry I now walk in.

She prophesied over me, saying, "God has called you to be a prophet to the nations." At the time, I didn't have a clue what that meant, but today, I get to see thousands upon thousands impacted by directive prophetic words that shape their lives. I am a seemingly insignificant person from a relatively poor background, a person of color born into apartheid-era South Africa. Yet, God places me on stages in front of thousands of people and in boardrooms alongside multibillionaires! That is the wisdom of God. No matter how big or how small you think your story is, God has an incredible plan and purpose to use you to impact many people. If we grab hold of who He is and who we are in Him, we get to live in an entirely new reality—a reality created through relationship with Him.

The gospel has changed and will forever change our planet and the universe. But while purposing to redeem the physical world, God's heart is deeply set upon changing lives one person at a time. He is interested in the individual story as much as He is in redeeming the cosmos. I finally understood this one day as I was reading scripture. I realized that names were recorded not just for history's sake, but because God chose to include individual names of women and men whose lives mattered to Him.

IN CHRIST, IN GLORY

Part of walking in our intrinsic creativity is not just understanding the power of our story but also how God sees us. Romans 3:23 tells us, "All have sinned and fallen short of the glory of God." Many of us need to be reminded that the work of salvation means the weight of this verse has now been reversed. Jesus has restored us to God's glory.[2] Glory is the revelation of the intrinsic worth and beauty of God, the divine excellence and unspoken manifestation of God. We have been restored to His divine excellence; we get to be people who carry His splendor and beauty.

God's desire, from the beginning of the world, was to create us as image-bearers who reveal His glory. Our essential worth is connected to who He is because we carry His divine splendor. The beautiful thing about salvation is that we have been put into Christ, and we are now in the same space that Jesus occupies in trinitarian intimacy because we are in Him. In Jesus Christ, God has given us access to the very heart of God.

One of the joys of coming into a relationship with Jesus is that the original intent of our nature is restored, and our original state is not sinful but Christlike. We were found in Christ before we were found in Adam. The Bible tells us this in Ephesians 1:3-4 when it says, "Blessed be the God and Father of our Lord Jesus Christ, who has blessed us in Christ with every spiritual blessing in the heavenly places, even as He chose us in Him before the foundation of the world, that we should be holy and blameless before Him."

Our perception of ourselves is incorrect if we see ourselves through the lens of who we were. This must change so that we know who we are *now*, in Christ. God's original intent for us was never to look like fallen Adam, but to look like His Son, Jesus Christ. Our state has changed. I no longer need to think through the lens of sin; I now think through the lens of my Christ-likeness, and my participation with Him.

You may recall the WWJD (What Would Jesus Do?) wristbands that were popular in the '90s. I was never a great fan of them because I would often look at them, asking, "What would Jesus do?" and thinking, *Probably not what I'm about to do...*

The reality is, we're not called just to be copies of Jesus. Salvation doesn't just mean we imitate Jesus. Salvation means we are joined to Him, and we have become participators in His very life—a life that demonstrated the kingdom while He was on Earth. I love how Terry Virgo puts it: "The same life that Jesus lived that was perfect and sinless, that demonstrated signs and wonders, that lifted the poor—everything that Jesus was and is, He gives to you as a gift called righteousness as if you lived that life yourself." That is what salvation means: we are participators in His life, not imitators only.

John 1 tells us that the Word was at the beginning, creating beauty out of nothing.[3] We are now partakers of that creative, divine nature[4] because of our union with Christ. That almost sounds blasphemous, but, because we are in Him, His nature has become our nature.

Jesus only needed to speak a word and things would happen or be created. God has called us to be creators enthused by the Spirit, whose words and actions co-create with His. That might challenge how you think about yourself, but by the spiritual DNA that is now in you, you are creative.

Your calling to participate in His creativity isn't dependent on your personality type or skill set—it's the reality of your New Creation being. Creativity is in your genes. It is part of you because you are part of Christ.

THE CREATOR-CREATED CREATIVES

God most clearly expresses our ability to create through our anatomy, by granting us the privilege of having children. This aspect of our nature was designed by God to reveal His desire for us to imitate His creativity. Humans partner with the Creator to create more of themselves. We know that all life comes from Him and is connected to Him, but we influence when this life manifests by determining when we procreate. The creation of life is, to this extent, dependent upon us! God is clearly very secure in that His sovereignty works alongside our free will. The Creator has created us to be creatives who shape our lives and spheres of influence by His creative power. He wants us to see that our creative nature exists to impact and reshape our world. I believe the time is now where God will pour out upon the church an ability to shift things on a tremendous scale. Consider the Renaissance, when the church was at the forefront of creativity as beautiful artwork was produced and the culture of the day was forever changed. It was the church that brought reformation to society and moved people out of the Dark Ages. We need creatives. We need people who dare to believe they can partner with God on the adventure of co-creating with Him.

Our ability for creativity is not insignificant, nor is it an optional extra to what we are called to do. Ephesians presents a radical prophetic view of who we are in this world. It is a manifesto of our place in the cosmos, describing our place in God's grand purpose on the earth. Creativity is essential to this purpose. We are seated in Christ, who is "far above all rule and authority and power and dominion . . . in this age"; God has "put all things under His feet," proclaiming Him "head over all things to the church."[5]

The God who calls us to work with Him is busy redeeming all things and bringing them under Christ. To partner with God means we get to be a part of re-creating and releasing newness over every aspect of the earth. This may seem overwhelming, but the letter to the Ephesians readies us for this role by praying that "the eyes of your heart"— also translatable as "imagination"—"may be enlightened in order that you may know the hope to which He has called you, the riches of His glorious inheritance in His holy people, and His incomparably great power for us who believe."[6]

This is the end of the longest sentence in the whole Bible. For comparison's sake, the shortest sentence is "Jesus wept." I wonder if even the length of the statements point us to the fact that, from God's perspective, the afflictions we experience are light and momentary compared to the glory He will reveal in us.

UNLOCKING YOUR IMAGINATION

Paul starts the letter to the Ephesians with worship as he prays what is called a *berakah*, a blessing in Jewish liturgy that creates an atmosphere of worship. Worship engages the imagination. And when imagination is unlocked in the context of worship, it's reoriented around the greatness of who God is. "Worship functions to renew the imagination, literally re-minding people of what is true and what really matters."[7] As the greatness of God is described and celebrated, we get to see who He is and what He can do. "Our worship is an act of spirit-led imagination that permits us to see and live differently; it is very upstream, against the grain of dominant reality."[8]

In Ephesians 1:17-20, Paul prays for the Spirit of wisdom and revelation to come, and for our hearts to understand our inheritance in Christ. In addition to our imagination, the eyes of our heart (verse 18) refer also to our decision-making and perception.

Paul prayed for the eyes of our heart to begin to see because he understood that the heart has eyes and is *able* to see. Paul desired that our ability to make decisions, to think, and to imagine would be unlocked. Ephesians 3:20 describes God as the One "who is able to do far more abundantly than all we ask or think." To "think" is also translated as "ask" or "imagine." God challenges us: "If you want to try to over-exaggerate my goodness, go ahead and imagine it, but I will still trump your imagination! I will go way above that!"

Imagination is the seedbed of faith. Your imagination is the blank check of faith that God gives you. If you can begin to imagine and see what God wants to do with your sphere of influence, you can have it.

Too often, the church has squashed imagination because we've bought into a "practical" concept of how life should work. Everything is in a box, everything is in its place, but God says, "I'm calling you to think like Me and begin to imagine like Me."

Here is a thought: imagination is so important to God that He created you out of His imagination. The Trinity—Father, Son, Holy Spirit—

discussed what it would look like for Them to create, and They imagined you! If we can engage our imagination, then what we see is what we can begin to have on the earth.

Imagine a world where human trafficking was eliminated. Imagine what it would look like if running water, electricity, food, and good education were given to the poor. Imagine a world where men and women are free to be entirely who they are meant to be. Imagine what it would look like for you to have kingdom impact on your family and in your workplace. Start imagining, because if you can see it with the eyes of faith, God wants to do even better than what you see. Bruggeman says it clearly in his book *Prophetic Imagination*:

> The imagination must come before the implementation. Our culture is competent to implement almost anything and to imagine almost nothing. The same royal consciousness that makes it possible to implement anything and everything is the one that shrinks imagination because imagination is a danger. Thus, every totalitarian regime is frightened of the artist. It is the vocation of the prophet to keep alive the ministry of imagination, to keep on conjuring and proposing futures alternative to the single one the king wants to urge as the only thinkable one.[9]

IMAGINATION AND INTELLECT

The only reason we do not value imagination is that we have valued logic and information over faith. As James K. A. Smith says, "What if the primary work of education is the transforming of our imagination rather than the saturation of our intellect?"[10] Information gathering does not produce expectation. Faith does not come by doing the sums. Faith does not come by working it all out. It is by faith that we understand that the world was created in one Word.[11]

The church Paul addressed in Ephesus started with an outpouring of the Holy Spirit, including many miracles, signs, and wonders. And it also began in a synagogue. The religious institution did not like what God was doing, as is often the case, so Paul moved from the "sacred place" of the synagogue to the "secular space" of the hall of Tyrannus. This meeting place of philosophers became a space where unusual miracles started happening, and, as a result of moving the sacred gospel into a public space, "all the residents of Asia heard the word of the Lord."[12]

In the hall of Tyrannus, Paul went after the thinkers and mind-molders of society. The gospel of Jesus is not an unintelligent gospel. It's not a blind faith but is intellectually satisfying as well as spiritually alive. It was never meant to be one or the other. The Bible says we are to understand this gospel and understand what God is doing.[13] Yet, understanding is not to be gained only through the gathering of information but, as is typical in Hebrew culture, also through experience.

John 8:32 says, "You will know the truth, and the truth will set you free." The word "know" is the Greek word *ginóskó*, which essentially means to come to an understanding through personal experience. This is why you can present truth to people and some will experience it and be changed, but others, while they understand it conceptually, do not experience a changed life.

Understanding and logic do not trump faith. Faith in the goodness of God is how we gain understanding and logic. Because we have worshiped at the altar of intellect and logic, we have diminished our senses and our spiritual intelligence, locking the realm of our imagination. We must begin to imagine again. Every single amazing event that has happened on planet Earth started in someone's imagination.

A Hebrew understood that God's inheritance for His people was not only healing or provision, but included the restoration of ruined cities and the establishment of things as God had always intended them to be.[14]

What are you imagining? What are you thinking about? We have to have dreams greater than just buying a beautiful house with a picket fence and two dogs. It's got to be about more than that! In the words of the great U2 singer, Bono, "Dream up the kind of world you want to live in. Dream out loud."

FAITH FOR THE IMPOSSIBLE

Imagination is the seedbed of faith, so when we start to live in the space of dreams and imaginings, we begin thinking about what God could do. This releases God's goodness to accomplish the impossible.

My story is a case in point: it is impossible for me to do what I do if I depend solely on my earthly pedigree. But I grew up dreaming about preaching in front of thousands of people. From the age of eight to twelve, I would fall asleep imagining myself preaching in specific churches. It has since come to pass that I have spoken in all of those churches! I imagined what I would be doing, where I would be preaching, and even miracles I would see. I envisioned myself doing all kinds of ministry. But there is nothing in me that qualified me for that. Instead, the thing that has given me the most distress in my life is the sound of my voice and my speech impediment. The weakest part of me, the thing that I thought disqualified me, is now the very thing that God uses to enable me to do what I imagined in my mind when I was an eight-year-old boy.

The author of the Message Bible, Eugene Peterson, emphasized the importance of imagination in a sermon:

> In our culture right now, the imagination is maybe the least developed faculty in adults. We let other people do our imagining for us, and as a culture, we take the lowest denominator of imagination. But the imagination is almost, not quite, the same thing as faith. It's that which connects what we see and what we don't see, and pulls us through what we see into what we don't see. Now, when that imagination involves trust and participation in the unseen, it's faith. But imagination is the training ground for that. That's why I think novelists, poets—we should ordain them. They are very important to the life of the faith, the life of the church.[15]

Your imagination is the gateway for the impossible. Some of you reading this have become disappointed that what you thought should happen has not happened. But be encouraged. If you can begin to see with the eyes of faith, if you start to imagine once more, God can do the impossible. What you see with the eyes of imagination sets the course for creative demonstrations of kingdom life.

You are a creation of trinitarian imagination. You exist as a result of being imagined by the Father, Son, and Holy Spirit. Being made in God's image means you, too, are able to create what your imagination conceives. Jesus said, "Truly, truly, I say to you, unless one is born again he cannot see the kingdom of God."[16] The word for "see" is the Greek *horaó*, meaning "to see with the mind." We are saved to perceive and imagine a world in which the kingdom is released and manifested. This is not about whimsical, wishful thinking. When we fill our imagination with the truth of our new identity as sons of the living God, there is no limit to what we can trust Him for.

IMAGINATION AND THE DECLARED WORD

Our lives are being phenomenally shaped by technological advancements. Years back, when the developers of tablets, smartphones, and software imagined the future, language was developed to communicate these devices' functions and capabilities. Using newly created terms—such as "apps," "tweets," "login," "posts," "blogs," and many more—shapes our daily realities.

I love what university Professor of Logic at Oxford University, Timothy Williamson, says[17] about imagination and language:

> Imagination creates a new language. Imagination can change the world because new ideas can change the world and it takes imagination to have a new idea. For example, in 1936, the logician Alan Turing published a paper where he imagines in precise detail a computing machine. It has a finite number of possible internal configurations, and scans an infinite tape one square at a time, writing or erasing symbols from a finite alphabet on the current square, moving to the next square, and changing its internal configuration, as determined by its current internal configuration and the currently scanned symbol, according to fixed rules.

Although Turing was not the first person to imagine some sort of calculating machine, his paper is generally regarded as the first appearance of the modern idea of a computer. In World War II, inspired by his imaginary machines, Turing had a real computing machine built that played an important part in decrypting German military and naval signals, and so in the defeat of Nazism. Computers have changed the world in obviously massive ways—and without them, you would not be reading these words. Turing's imagination changed the world.

I wonder: if more Christians engaged our imaginations in Jesus, how could we change the world? What is your imagination set upon?

When you marry imagination with the power of declaration, realities are created. We have the ability to speak words in which the kingdom of God is made manifest. The words of God in the mouth of Jesus are as powerful as the words of God in your mouth. What do I mean by that? Wherever Jesus went, He ministered by being aware of the unseen reality of God's kingdom. We, too, reflect the reality we are most aware of.

Jesus lived with the reality of heaven. When He saw someone who was sick, He merely spoke a word that carried power to create what He declared. To the man with the withered hand, He said, "Stretch out your hand." Words with inherent power enabled the man to do what he could not do before.

Your words also create realities. Peter understood this. He saw Jesus merely speak a word and raise the dead. Peter saw Jesus speak a word and heal people. He saw how Jesus released the kingdom through the power of a declared kingdom word. Consequently, in Matthew 14, when the disciples were caught in a storm and saw Jesus walking on water, it was Peter who was prepared to walk on water. But he first required Jesus to speak to him.[18] Peter understood that the words Jesus spoke carried power, in and of themselves, to create new realities. When Jesus proclaimed the gospel, it became an event to be entered into. In other words, kingdom experience was available in the word that was announced. As we saw previously, George Eldon Ladd put it this way: "The Kingdom was present not only in deed but also in word. The word which Jesus proclaimed itself brought to pass that which it proclaimed: release for the captives, recovery for the blind, freeing of the oppressed." Ladd goes on to quote Friedrich: "The message creates the new era, it makes possible the signs of messianic fulfillment. The word brings about the Kingdom of God."[19]

In essence, when you agree with heaven and declare words in faith, those words carry power to create the reality they describe. This is not simply positive thinking. Positive thinking requires work in order to believe in what is being said. There is power in the declared word, however, to manifest that which you think, imagine, or trust God for, because your words are in cooperation with heaven itself. This is why Jesus told the woman caught in adultery, "Go and sin no more." It was not a rebuke but empowerment: His spoken word was empowering her to live a life free of sin. They were words with the power to shape her and her future. Jesus spoke with such authority that His very words proclaimed the presence of the new age of the kingdom.

Your words also have power because you are a co-creator with Jesus—you are joined to Him. When we declare new realities, we demonstrate the fact that we are made in God's image, because that is how the Father created all things: by His spoken word. In the place of darkness, God said, "Let there be light," and it was so. Our declarations release creativity.

You can do the same when faced with what may seem to be impenetrable difficulties. When the kingdom of God does not seem present, you can demonstrate the kingdom by joining with heaven and speaking a new reality. Jesus ministered out of being aware of the unseen reality of His Father's world. If we can understand and learn to be mindful of the co-existing reality of heaven, then we will be able to shift the atmospheres around us. What heaven looks like is meant to be revealed here on Earth.

LEARNING TO REIMAGINE

Once, I went into a meeting with several wealthy people, and I was quite intimidated. One person was dripping in gold, another had two private jets, and together their collective wealth was more than the GDP of South Africa. I questioned myself. How was I to minister to them? As I entered the boardroom, the Lord said to me, "Son, I want you to remember that you are the wealthiest person in this room." That seemed in direct contrast to the situation, but I considered the reality of heaven, where there is no lack, only abundance, and that changed the way I saw myself. When I began to speak, I commanded the attention of some of the most influential people in the world, because I understood my identity in Christ.

I am learning to reimagine my world and my place in it. I am learning to re-create the world around me. I am learning that, because of my union with Christ, God has invested creative power in me so that what I speak releases the kingdom. This is what Jesus did when He said, "The Kingdom of God is at hand."[20] Jesus was declaring that there was a new reality. He was saying, "The future age of My rule and reign is here now. It has broken in. Get ready, because what's about to happen will demonstrate that reality."

Do you realize who and whose you are? Do you understand that no matter what difficulty or challenge you're facing, you have the upper hand?

What are you thinking about? What are you imagining? What are you dreaming about? What words are you releasing?

You might find it very difficult to be positive in your current situation or location; this is true of South Africa, where I am from. The political and social injustice seems overwhelming there, but I am seeing God's kingdom manifest in those places as, little by little, He is bringing change. I choose to see that the kingdom of God is breaking in to make South Africa look more like heaven. I have to continually ask myself what I am agreeing with, what I am imagining and declaring over my city and my country. That's what will be released in and through me.

Ephesians 1:22-23 tells us, "And He put all things under His feet and gave Him as head over all things to the church, which is His body, the fullness of Him who fills all in all." What are the things under Jesus' feet? All things. That includes everything past, present, and future. It includes society, commerce, health, media—everything!

Jesus is the head of the church, His body, and He has given all things to the church to steward. The way the body of Christ will "fill all in all" is through you and me impacting all in all. This requires that we move away from living as if we are waiting for the rapture, to living as sons and daughters called to release kingdom and creativity on the earth.

What do you imagine this to look like? What we certainly are not trying to do is make all things look like a Sunday morning church meeting. We are not trying to create a Christian culture or impose religion on the world. We want to shape culture with heaven's government and influence, to make it easy for the broken, the hurting, and the dying to come into the kingdom. We do not want to Christianize anything; we want to establish God's kingdom, because when you establish God's kingdom, people fall into His love and His grace.

In my first job, one of the things that I felt God say to me was not to tell anyone that I was a Christian. For the first four months, I didn't tell anyone about my faith; I just lived life really well. I began to speak words of life into the atmosphere—it was quite an anxious atmosphere, as our boss was highly strung (I don't think I have ever heard as many expletives as I did that year). But, after about four or five months, my line manager said to me, "What is it about you that makes me think about eternity?" He was not a Christian, did not go to church, and I had not told him I was a Christian. My internal world had created a reality around me for him to encounter.

On another occasion, I was in a pub in the United Kingdom when a lady who had been involved in the occult approached me and said, "What is it about you? You shine so brightly." While I was hoping it was not because of oily skin, she said, "I've never seen such pure light around anyone." What I carry in me will always spill over around me, no matter where I am.

God's kingdom in you is meant to infiltrate the world around you. If you can begin to imagine it, if you can start to dream, if you can start to join with the co-creative power of heaven in you and on you, you can redefine the reality around you by how you live and by what you say. Jesus directly spoke words so revolutionary, they turned the Middle East upside down. We can do the same.

What are you imagining? What are you declaring? To see God do the extraordinary, you must begin to fill your imagination with His thoughts. Reimagine your world and join heaven in re-creating the world for His purposes.

---

1. Genesis 45:8
2. John 17:22
3. John 1:1-3
4. 2 Peter 1:4
5. Ephesians 1:21-22
6. Ephesians 1:18-19
7. Timothy G. Gombis, *The Drama of Ephesians: Participating in the Triumph of God* (p. 67 of Kindle Edition, 2010).
8. Walter Brueggemann, *Mandate to Difference: An Invitation to the Contemporary Church*, n.p.
9. Walter Bruggeman, *The Prophetic Imagination*, p. 40.
10. James K. A. Smith, *Desiring the Kingdom (Cultural Liturgies): Worship, Worldview, and Cultural Formation* (Baker Academic, 2009), p. 18.
11. Hebrews 11:3
12. Acts 19:10
13. 1 Chronicles 12:32
14. Isaiah 61:4
15. https://www.youtube.com/watch?v=Faalui7cESs (27 min and 19 sec in)
16. John 3:3
17. https://www.bigquestionsonline.com/2013/06/25/how-can-imagination-change-world/
18. Matthew 14:28
19. George Eldon Ladd, *The Presence of the Future*, n.p.
20. Matthew 4:17

05
Spiritual Intelligence

"But we have the mind of Christ."

1 Corinthians 2:16

I found myself, one day, sitting in an office in a skyscraper. I had been asked to consult prophetically for a multinational company, meeting with some high-flying executives who needed prophetic direction and destiny coaching. To say I was nervous or felt under-qualified is an understatement. Yet, this has become an increasingly familiar experience for me.

My invitations to contexts like this aren't because of a prophetic gifting or even because I have a skill set that these influential people need. Instead, it's because I am convinced we can engage the mind of Christ in any situation and gain heavenly insight that will help unlock destiny. The prophetic does not just work in the church context. In that meeting, I got to prophesy over one of the company's executives and see him encounter Jesus as the Holy Spirit revealed the secrets of his heart and the mysteries of God's heart for him and his family. All I did was lean into the kind thoughts Jesus had for him and begin to share them with him. There was no atmosphere of worship, no sense of power on me. It was a simple conviction that God loves to speak to me and wants to speak to anyone I come in contact with.

In Christ, you carry heaven's power to redeem all things so that wherever you show up, that space becomes holy. God wants to help you discover how He speaks to you, how to act on what He says, and how to seize the moments of His favor that come your way. When we're oriented to see that God is involved in every moment of our day, we get to partner with Him in everything we do.

The way we do this is by learning how to recognize His voice and see His fingerprints. I call this spiritual intelligence.

UNLOCKING SPIRITUAL INTELLIGENCE IN YOUR DAILY LIFE

Throughout scripture, God uses men and women who know the promises of God and who recognize the leading of the Spirit. They identify the moments when the Spirit and promises converge, and they engage them to experience personal blessing and the advancement of God's kingdom. This ability to connect the dots, which comes by the supernatural endowment of the Holy Spirit, appeared irregularly under the Old Covenant. In the New Covenant, however, this takes place by the indwelling presence of the Holy Spirit, who gives us access to the thoughts and intentions of Christ all the time!

Because of dualistic thinking that sees the spiritual as separate from the physical, we carry an expectation that spiritual experiences are predominantly relegated to church meetings. When we realize that spiritual encounters and directives are not just for church meetings, everything becomes an opportunity for redemption. The way we do business, recreation, friendship, problem-solving, and family is to be infused with a spirituality that demonstrates His kingdom. Becoming aware of spiritual reality in our everyday life helps us recognize God's involvement in everything.

Spiritual intelligence is the ability to perceive the unseen reality of God's world engaging with our world. This is what happened with Elisha's servant: "And Elisha prayed, 'Open his eyes, LORD, so that he may see.' Then the LORD opened the servant's eyes, and he looked and saw the hills full of horses and chariots of fire all around Elisha."[1]

Heaven's reality is available to every Christian. It gives us the advantage, setting us up for a place of influence and favor—if we steward well the moments God gives us. When you begin to partner with heaven in the marketplace, the school, the studio, or wherever you find yourself, a whole new world of opportunity opens up to you. A close friend told me how God began to show him how to position himself for opportunities that he was not qualified for. Consequently, he climbed the corporate ladder in an accelerated way directly because he developed his spiritual intelligence. Spiritual intelligence flows from learning to engage with the mind of Christ every day and at any moment.

Spiritual intelligence also allows you to recognize how God is at work in difficult and challenging situations. I invite you to partner with God in those moments and co-create with Him so that you see His preferred future for you come to pass. This will help you to navigate life so that long-held, seemingly impossible prophetic words come to fruition.

Many people of significance in the Bible recognized these moments. Think of barren Sarah, stuttering Moses, the slave Joseph, and the young Jewish girl Esther who defied the odds set against her in a male-dominated world. The list carries on: Daniel, raised up while a captive in an evil regime; Amos, the farmer who prophesied in the midst of despair; and of course, Jesus, who was born under a scandalous cloud of illegitimacy into a poor household, considered the least in His Jewish context, with no real hope of doing anything significant. Yet God raised them all up. This can be true of you, too!

Jesus' ministry on the earth is an example of how we can live. His story is now our story. His ministry is now our ministry. What strikes me about this is that the incredible ministry He demonstrated was hardly ever done in what was known as a "sacred place." Most of His teachings, miracles, and demonstrations of power happened in the context of homes, work environments, the marketplace, and the outdoors. Jesus demonstrated the kingdom of God wherever He was, and most of the time He did not remain in a temple but was among the people.

In Luke 6, Jesus healed a man with a withered hand on the Sabbath. Luke tells us that the Pharisees tried to catch Jesus out on the subtler points of the Law. They wanted to set Him up for failure in order to have a reason to punish Him and discredit His ministry. But Jesus knew their thoughts because of spiritual intelligence. He was able not only to heal on the Sabbath but also to answer the Pharisees and expose their evil intentions. Jesus was able to perceive what they were thinking ahead of time. As a result, He demonstrated the love of God in healing this poor man, yet kept His credibility and influence despite the Pharisees' attack. That is a powerful tool to have when in challenging situations.

In Luke 5:1-7, Jesus, a carpenter, instructed fishermen who'd been working the whole night on where to cast their nets. Their obedience to His word resulted in such a large catch of fish that they didn't have enough nets to retrieve it all. The economic impact that such a catch would have on their respective families was significant. Jesus, by revelation, got insight as to when and where the fishermen could get the catch of their lives. Spiritual intelligence gives us that kind of insight. It helps us connect the dots leading to a moment of favor, a moment in which those around us experience the King and His kingdom.

HEARING TO LISTEN

Our society bombards us with noise and voices that drown out the sound of heaven, but it's in the busyness of life that God wants to speak. In the midst of noise, we need to learn to tune in to His voice.

I love the prophetic. I love moments when God sets us up to connect the dots in what He's doing so that it brings people into an experience with a very kind Father. I believe God wants to use all of us, in any kind of context, because God wants to influence our lives and worlds with His thoughts, ideas, and creativity. I'm hearing stories more often about people who've begun sensing God's presence because they're developing their spiritual intelligence, their discernment of what God is doing and saying. They've learned to dust for His fingerprints even in moments outside of church buildings or worship settings. They understand God has placed them in significant places of favor.

Part of walking in spiritual intelligence is learning to listen for God's voice. We know that God speaks to us in various ways, but when we struggle to hear Him, it's often not our hearing that's impaired but our ability to listen. Listening requires going beyond hearing to understanding what's being said.

When Isaiah 11:2 speaks about "the spirit of understanding," the word for "understanding" means consideration and discernment, tools that enable you to penetrate to the heart of a matter. God wants us to receive His words so that we hear His heart.

Hebrews 1:2 tells us that God "has spoken to us by His Son." The Greek word for "by" is the preposition "in." God speaks to us in His Son. His language begins in sonship. Just like we may speak English or French, God's language is sonship.

Sonship in Hebrew carries three distinct aspects. To be a son means that you carry and share the same nature of the Father—your life is directly sourced from the life-giving nature of the Father. The second aspect is that you reflect and resemble the Father. This speaks of your purpose: to reveal and resemble the Father's character. The last aspect of sonship is that you are an heir to the Father's riches. This is the reward of the Father. All of these come to us by grace through all Jesus did on the cross.

The starting point for listening to God is sonship. I have to learn how to be a good son to a Father who wants to lavish His goodness on me and speak to me out of His kindness.

WALKING IN SONSHIP

I recently had coffee with a colleague who confessed to me that he felt trapped by the will of God. Having received numerous words from God, he felt under pressure to make them happen—he had stepped out of sonship and onto the treadmill of performance. This is the wrong mindset and approach to seeing the prophetic promises of God work themselves out. Spiritual intelligence does not look like performance. It must come from a place of rest in knowing that God has chosen to partner with us to see His will come to pass in our lives.

Listening to God and being sensitive to His movements are not about receiving our daily orders. Instead, His words are invitations for us to enjoy our sonship. Exciting as this may be, I have sadly found that for many in the church, understanding what it means to be a son is a great obstacle.

Instead of dishing out orders, our Father is inviting us to dream with

Him. In Matthew 10:39, Jesus' words to His disciples "to lose their lives" may seem like an order from the commander-in-chief, but this is God's call to us to truly find who we were created to be, and it leads to His gift of "abundant life."[2]

In the prior verse, Jesus says we're to pick up our crosses and follow Him. This is often interpreted as "death to self," as if our personality and gift set have to die. I don't know if you've ever understood that our old nature, our old self, did, subsequently, *die as instructed* on the cross with Jesus. Everything that blocked off a radical relationship with God was nailed on the cross in Christ.

We now live in the reality of sonship. So, when Jesus says, "Pick up your cross," it's not about inviting in pain and despair but the promise of resurrection life. Far from saying, "Become a worm in the sand," or, "You're worth nothing," He's saying, "All of the promises embodied in the cross and resurrection are yours now to carry." He's saying, "It's your turn to reveal the Father." Now, isn't that more exciting?

The cross is the place of victory and life, because it's in our union with Jesus in His death that we find resurrection life. If we died with Him, then we have been raised with Him too. This is not a future event but a reality for us now. It's in this process that we find who we really are and who God really is.

Notice that Jesus is God's only *begotten* Son. I love this emphasis on "begotten" because it's a clue that there may be other types of sons waiting in the wings. We are God's *adopted* sons, and God has, in His infinite creativity, put in each of us a personality that is unique, just as He did in Jesus.

God has placed a unique set of gifts in you, and He wants to develop your unique way of connecting with Him. Your past, experiences, and life are not meant to be squashed or erased out of the way; they're to be redeemed so He can use them for His glory. We can trust that God doesn't want to crush who we are because it's only in Christ that we fully discover our humanity, and it's only through Christ that we fully find out who we are meant to be. As C. S. Lewis said, "We have, in our day, started by getting the whole picture upside down. Starting with the doctrine that every individual is 'of infinite value,' we then picture God as a kind of employment committee whose business it is to find suitable careers for souls, square holes for square pegs. In fact, however, the value of the individual does not lie in him. He is capable of receiving value. He receives it by union with Christ."[3]

When you begin to understand that your life in Christ isn't one that merely imitates Him but one that participates and shares in His life—so that you become entirely who you are meant to be—then scripture becomes an invitation to search the unsearchable, to enter into and explore the very depths of God.

QUALIFIED FOR THE EXTRAORDINARY

A few years ago, I was asked to pray for a lady who could not fall pregnant. I felt God show me a doctor's report and I sensed what was wrong with this lady. I don't have any medical training or qualification that would enable me to deduce or make any kind of diagnosis, but I said, "This is your problem, and I think you should go back to your doctor and tell him this is your problem." She went back, had my diagnosis confirmed, and was able to fall pregnant. Here's my point: God has a habit of surprising us where we feel least qualified. As you develop a track record with Him, you discover who He is and how He thinks so that the intellectual property of heaven becomes yours—as scripture says it is.

I have a friend who's possibly one of the most unqualified people to be working in a business context, but God spoke to him about maneuvering himself into the trajectory of divine favor to get him into places where he could never get himself. And everything in his mind would've said, "You should not go there because you're not qualified to go there." But when you're beginning to develop spiritual intelligence, when you're starting to develop an understanding that God wants to use the ordinary and everyday—the mundane of your life—to be appointed to His purpose, then what would take you many years can happen in a moment.

God wants to release creativity in people so that they come up with more than just another nice thing, but rather, ideas that begin to reshape culture. And He wants to do that primarily by helping you develop an internal reality that's awakened to Him. When God's inviting you to search out the unsearchable, I encourage you to search out that which is hidden in Him. And before anyone accuses me of being gnostic—Gnosticism being the desire to look for something beyond Jesus, as if there is more than Jesus—the reality is, while Jesus is everything we need, He is a mystery that is yet to be unfolded and discovered: "He has a name written, that no one knows, but himself."[4]

You and I can have our spiritual intelligence unlocked by a Jesus who, in any context, in any crowd, could figure out what was really happening. Whether He was healing a man with a withered hand while seeing through the Pharisees' traps, or walking as the carpenter past some fishermen and saying, "Throw your net on the other side," He operated in the fullness of God's wisdom. I don't know how many of you like to take advice in your particular profession from someone who has no clue about it, but the financial result of obedience for those fishermen meant that they had to call other boats to come and gather the fish. Imagine what it was like at the market that day when they sold their catch.

We often disqualify ourselves because we view ourselves through the lens of our natural ability, placing our intelligence quota above the empowering presence of the Holy Spirit. In reality, it is the Holy Spirit who releases spiritual intelligence—answers, ideas, and thoughts that can bring incredible breakthrough to people.

I have friends to whom God speaks through dreams so significant that governments and heads of state phone them before making decisions; they ask them to dream or to hear from God on their behalf. This is the reality we get to enter into right now. I often get to sit with business leaders and help shape the culture of their companies, bringing prophetic words of destiny into their lives. All I'm doing is learning how to use my spiritual intelligence and repackaging it in a language that makes it accessible.

My friend Richard shares his story of spiritual intelligence. He translates what God does with him in the sacred space and how it spills over into the public place. Here is his story:

Some years ago, I was in a prophetic meeting, and I remember being a bit wowed about what was happening, because God was marking people radically around the room. I was relatively conservative, and the preacher came up to the front and started declaring and releasing different callings over the place. He began by saying, "I see a mantel of pastoring coming over; I see a mantel of worship coming over; I see a mantel of apostolic coming over." Different people were getting marked by the radical presence of God, and I remember being a little bit uncomfortable because I hadn't seen anything this charismatic; I hadn't seen the move of the Spirit like that before. And then he finally said, "Okay, I'm going to release one more thing, and it's only going to touch a few people in the room. And if it isn't you, I want you to get out of the way of these people." So I thought, *Okay, I'm getting out of the way!* So he says, "It's coming on one, two, three!" And he says, "I release a mantel of signs and wonders." I remember the power of God came on me for the first time in my life in such an ecstatic way, I flew back a couple rows of chairs.

So, maybe some of you are like, "You know, I'm longing for an encounter with the Lord." Me? I was not that person. I was not looking for that. And I got radically arrested by the goodness and the grace and the favor of God, and I went into this ecstatic encounter with God. It lasted, at first, for about four hours. The Lord would start to encounter me; angels would come and visit me. And then it extended for another seven days, where I would just shake under the power of God, and the heat of His presence would come on me, and I would only be able to sleep for about three hours a night. The angels would visit me in the night, and I remember thinking that I was losing my mind. But I'd never felt so desperately and wildly in love with Jesus.

I was doing my Master's degree at the time in encryption/decryption, and I was working with the military in engineering, and I'd come to a stop. I'd come to a block. Just to give you context: I think sixteen people started the Master's degree, and there ended up being only two people who finished. It was difficult. And I remember, I'd just come to a block. My wife and I were dating at the time, and I remember saying to her, "I think I'm just going to quit." And that night—it was about two or three weeks after this radical encounter—I went to bed, and as I was sleeping, an angel of the Lord came and visited me. He gave me a scroll, and as I opened it up, the Lord said, "This is a telecommunications algorithm, and it's for your Master's degree." I remember opening up the scroll and reading, and it said, "AODV" on the scroll, and I had no idea what it was.

Then I woke up out of the dream in a cold sweat, and I remember going to the computer and researching what this algorithm was. It turned out to be Ad-hoc On-demand Distance Vector, which is the shortest path of telecommunication algorithm for telecoms. And it became the cornerstone of my dissertation and my Master's degree.

I ended up going on to publish a book on that technology. I still worked hard on it—it was a key the Lord gave me—but I got to a place where I mathematically modeled these simulations, and I'd be stuck modeling the telecommunication algorithm. While I'd be stuck, I'd actually go and fall back asleep, and that same angel of the Lord would visit me and pass me a scroll. I'd wake up in the morning, and I'd be able to work out the mathematical modeling simulation.

It wasn't just favor on my natural ability; I'm a smart guy, but I'm not the cleverest guy. This wasn't just my innate ability. I had this moment of encounter where the Lord marked me, and then it actually caused me to step into favor that was beyond myself and my ability. I went on to publish that book, and it got published internationally—I think about six times—in China, America, Denmark. One moment that took me by surprise was the second time I was published. I was attending the National Military Convention in a certain country, and I was placed next to the keynote speaker of the event, the Indian foreign minister of defense. I remember sitting there; I was wearing a suit with a sunflower and still had dreadlocks. I was sitting there with the head of the army, the head of the navy, the head of the air force, UK defense representative, U.S. defense representative, the foreign minister of defense for India, and other foreign ministers of defense for different nations. I thought, *I'm dreadlocked up, sunflower on my suit. Lord, this is Your grace, and this is Your favor. And I had a moment with You that opened doors of favor that I could never have stepped through if it was just my skill and ability or hard work.*

What is beautiful is that this story can be imparted. I remember the first time I ever shared this story, I was with a group of CEOs and high-level earners in America, and I started impartation with them. There was a man from Chicago who had a connection with the Forex in a particular country, and I remember praying impartation with him that the Lord would encounter him.

A few weeks later, I got in contact with him, and he said the wildest thing happened. Now, this is a heady guy. This is a guy who's involved in business at a high level, not one of these ecstatic, mystic type of Christians. He said he was sitting in Starbucks, and while he was sitting, this cloud opened up in the spirit, and this algorithm started to write out in the sky. He said he'd never had any moment like that before, and he started to write it down. As he wrote it down, the Lord said, "This is the Forex algorithm." So he built a business around this Forex algorithm, and he ended up making millions in the process.

I believe that we're all chosen to step into favor. I'm on a journey where I'm like, "You know what? If this radical, prophetic, ecstatic expression of the Lord Jesus is true, it can't just be for closed church meetings." It can't just be for these meetings where we worship and we feel the presence of God. It can't just be where you get a prophetic word, and you see someone trembling under the power of God in these church meetings.

What if the angels started to step into the boardroom? What if the angels began to step in when you're sitting around with friends at a coffee shop and start dreaming up business ideas? What if the Lord started to step in and actually give you solutions? What if, while you're sitting down and dreaming about changing the city, the Lord starts to come, and He begins to prophesy destiny over that?

I've been on a journey where I've been experimenting with my businesses. I've said, "You know what? I don't want to just do it through my own skill and ability and working hard." I work hard, but I actually want to introduce and bring in the principles of the favor of God, bring in the prophetic, bring it into my business place and see if it will actually produce fruit, favor, clientele, income, and influence. And, wow, we have been seeing the most radical things happen—to the point now where we're stewarding three businesses, and the Lord's been so gracious and so amazing.

God is inviting you to use spiritual intelligence in your everyday life.

The problem is, the Western construct of society is far too busy. We have to become people who learn to listen a bit more and engage God's presence even when it's inconvenient. I've begun to discover that friendship with God is one of the most inconvenient things ever, because He loves interrupting my normal day. And if I can learn how to recognize when He interrupts, how to identify the moment of favor, recognize His fingerprints on a particular deal, a specific conversation, a relationship, then I can lean into His interruptions and turn them into moments of destiny, not just for me, but also for those I'm serving.

---

1. 2 Kings 6:17
2. John 10:10
3. C. S. Lewis, *The Weight of Glory* (Grand Rapids, 1974), pp. 41-42.
4. Revelation 19:12

06
Developing Spiritual Intelligence

"As for these four youths, God gave them learning and skill in all literature and wisdom, and Daniel had understanding in all visions and dreams."

Daniel 1:17

Your whole life, from the day that you were born until now, God has been teaching you how to hear His voice and walk in the supernatural. The things you've studied, the experiences you've had—some of them not God-ordained—God uses to set you up for success. Isn't that incredible?

KNOW THE VALUE OF YOUR EXPERIENCES

Sometimes we think that God ordains evil things to happen to us because He often shows up in the mess and turns it into something good. We conclude that maybe it was God's will. That is a misrepresentation of His goodness. God is always good; He's not going to send anything terrible to you.

His sovereignty does not mean that He's going to get you into failure and difficulty and suffering just to teach you a lesson. But He sure is good at showing up in the midst of challenges, taking what looks like an absolute disaster and turning it around for your good. He really, really is. I can tell you story after story about that.

The thing is, whether your experiences were God-ordained or not, He wants to use everything in your life as an opportunity to hear His voice, see His face, and engage with His heart. You've studied what you've studied because God wants to use you in that area. He wants you to access that knowledge as He uses you to impact the world around you. God wants to use your experience in life.

God uses my experience of growing up in apartheid South Africa as a sign and a wonder to many people. At just the age of twenty-two, I was called out into the northern suburbs of Cape Town to pray for a military man who was one of the apartheid government's key assassins. He targeted many of South Africa's freedom fighters, those fighting to end apartheid and racial divisions in our country. God chose to use a person of color to bring freedom to a racist. Well, he was an ex-racist after our prayer time! That is the beauty of the gospel. I was born for this! You were born into your body, skin color, family, and other dynamics because God wants to use those variables to reach the world—don't deny Him that opportunity! When you recognize that your whole life is a set-up for God's favor, even the negative stuff becomes an opportunity for redemption in your life and the lives of those you encounter.

RECOGNIZE THE SUPERNATURAL

Developing spiritual intelligence begins with understanding that, very often, the natural is an opportunity to lean into the supernatural. When it comes to hearing God's voice, many Christians think they're going to hear a deep, booming voice from heaven—like Sean Connery with a Scottish accent speaking in King James English, "Thus saith the Lord."

That's not how God speaks. Instead, God wants to use your natural experiences and make them supernatural.

Consider Moses walking in the desert. I have been in a desert in the Middle East: it's hot stuff. Then there's a burning bush. I don't think a burning bush is that uncommon. In fact, it could be deemed reasonably natural in a desert. But something happened when he walked past this common burning bush. And he stopped, and, the Bible says, "He looked, and behold, the bush was burning, yet it was not consumed. And Moses said, 'I will turn aside to see this great sight, why the bush is not burned.'"[1] Any other burning bush, and Moses would have carried on. But at the moment he stopped and looked again at that bush, he realized that the bush was not being consumed by the fire. That, my friends, is not natural.

God is speaking to us, all around us, all the time. The problem is, many of us don't stop to "look again" at our natural surroundings, and we miss the moment when God is speaking. When you learn to look again, when you learn to lean into God's purposes, the natural suddenly becomes alive with the supernatural.

In John 12, a voice spoke to Jesus from heaven, in the hearing of a crowd of people. Three types of responses arose from bystanders. Some people said, "Oh, it just thundered," and they took what was supernatural and reduced it to something very common. Sometimes God wants to speak to us, but because we don't have the right filter, we don't recognize Him. We rationalize His supernatural presence using our natural understanding.

Other bystanders said, "No, it's an angel that's speaking from heaven." People can believe in the supernatural without necessarily seeing the hand of God in it. They encounter the supernatural realm but don't encounter the Creator of everything both natural and supernatural. But Jesus spoke and clarified the matter for everyone present: "No, this is My Father in heaven."

Here's my point: when you begin to lean into God, there'll be moments when God will speak or leave fingerprints all over a deal, a relationship, the sudden resolution of a problem, and you'll have an opportunity to ignore that or to engage with it. One of the things I'm learning to do is to train my senses to engage with what God is doing and saying.[2] You've got a physical body that God wants to act through.

Sometimes, when I'm speaking to someone, my right or left hand suddenly warms up, and I'll think, *What is going on?* I've begun to recognize that this is my love language with God. I then often ask Him, "God, what's going on? It's very hot suddenly; what's going on? It's not a hot day. I'm in an air-conditioned room. Why are my hands suddenly burning?" As with a bush that burns but isn't consumed, warm hands in an air-conditioned room are a signal that the supernatural is breaking through the natural at that moment. This is how opportunities to pray for the sick present themselves to me. People get healed instantly.

It's so simple: when you live in constant awareness of His world, then you begin to recognize Him breaking into your world. That, right there, is called spiritual intelligence.

CULTIVATE YOUR HEART

We also develop spiritual intelligence by cultivating a soft heart. The Bible talks about this in Luke 8, where it discusses different kinds of ground we encounter when planting a seed. Jesus told His disciples that "The seed is the word of God." We see all different kinds of ground in this parable: hard ground, ground that is overrun with thorns. The seeds—the word of God—only survive when planted in the good soil. God's word impacts our lives, grows, and bears fruit when we cultivate our hearts to receive it. One of the things I've discovered is that if I don't cultivate the garden within my heart, it makes it hard for me to recognize the moments when God drops words into my life.

How do we cultivate our hearts to hear and recognize God's voice? I start by filtering what's coming into my heart, because I refuse to allow the world around me to dominate my thought life. I'm not talking about being super religious and avoiding TV or all things "secular." I'm just saying that what you allow in, unfiltered, will dominate your ability to recognize when God is breaking in, and that will stunt your spiritual intelligence.

I'm learning how to do this every single day, and the Lord keeps showing me new ways to cultivate my heart. This is especially profound in the context of parenthood. My wife and I are having this incredible time with our little boy, teaching him how to grow into a healthy child. In the process, we are learning that the impact of TV, iPads, and media upon the brain-development of a child can be quite destructive at a certain age. That got me thinking. I wonder if that's true of adults, too? We so often allow stuff in, unfiltered and unchecked, that when God breaks in, we don't have a grid to recognize Him. We have to learn to silence the world around us.

So much of our world is cluttered with noise. We're bombarded with notifications, DMs, PMs, tweets, retweets, ads, likes, shares, and—well, you get the picture. Not all of the noise is irrelevant, however, and so we must learn to hone in on the information—the words—that matter. We learn to let our thoughts and hearts be fed by the words, images, and ideas that bring life and inspiration.

Rather than get bogged down in the culture of comparison and opinion—which is easy to do when it surrounds us on all sides—I choose to cultivate a soft heart by living a life free of offense. You cannot offend me because, as my friend once said, "Offense is never given; it's always taken." By choosing not to take offense, I remain unoffendable, and my heart remains ready to access God's voice.

Not only that but I've begun to understand something: my heart needs to be pliable continually, and that flexibility comes out of a place of worship. And I'm not talking about just having some quiet time. I'm talking about enjoying God because He wants to be enjoyed by us.

Is your heart pliable and prepared to hear from God? Your heart is going to determine your ability to walk in spiritual intelligence.

MEDITATE ON GOD'S GOODNESS

Last, we develop our spiritual intelligence by studying and meditating upon biblical encounters. The Bible is full of incredible encounters: deep, mystical experiences with God that go beyond our comprehension but speak to our spirits. As you study them, you can't help but ask God to do it again. Our hearts cry out, "If you did it for Ezekiel, that he could see wheels within wheels, and if an angel appeared for Moses, won't you do this for me, too?" It is these biblical encounters that form the foundation of our desire to encounter God in our own lives.

We must learn to meditate on our own encounters, and develop a diary of God encounters. Memorialize the moments when God has spoken to you, or joined the dots for you, because very often those memorials point the way to where He will speak to you again.

When you develop that kind of secret place of celebrating what God is doing—instead of focusing on what He's *not* doing—it makes it easier for you to recognize moments and engage your spiritual senses to anticipate when God's kingdom will break out. Friends, you need to develop memorials of God's goodness. When things get tough, it's those memorials that keep us standing. If He could do it then, surely

He will do it now.

---

1. Exodus 3:2-3
2. Hebrews 5:14: "But solid food is for the mature, for those who have their powers of discernment trained by constant practice to distinguish good from evil."

07

Prophetic Personalities

"My sheep hear my voice, and I know them, and they follow me."

John 10:27

As we seek to walk in spiritual intelligence, many of us struggle to hear God's voice because we don't actually understand how God speaks to us specifically. God wants to use our personalities, who we are, to communicate to us. He wants to harness who we are so that we recognize Him in the moments we need to hear Him.

It is important to note that when you recognize how God speaks to you in your moment of favor, you get the opportunity to grab hold of that moment and allow God to take you into the places you least expect. Sometimes we miss favor because we have not learned to recognize the primary ways that God speaks to us.

MODES OF REVELATION AND PROPHETIC PERSONALITIES

The modes of revelation are the varied ways in which God speaks to us. For example, scripture, visions, the still small voice, and uncanny coincidences are all modes of revelation. I discuss this in more depth in my book *Gaining Heaven's Perspective* and in my mentoring course, Amplify (visit frequentsee.org/resources for more information).

Often, as Christians, we compartmentalize the moments when God speaks to us—thinking His voice and Word should arrive in a specific way—and miss His involvement in the everyday parts of our lives. We expect Him to speak during a worship service or a devotional time. This is good and right, but this way of relating to God and His voice becomes our default because we don't yet understand how *we* hear from Him. God does not just want to speak to you in church services and prayer meetings. He wants to speak in your everyday moments: in your worship, your work, and your recreation.

After more than 20 years of ministry in the prophetic, I am convinced that the issue of understanding God's voice in our daily lives is less about the mode in which we receive His revelation and more about how we recognize and process that revelation. I have ministered to many different people, and each encounter reveals how God speaks so uniquely to each of His children. Words, thoughts, or ideas that would mean nothing to me prove to have a profound impact on someone else. It wasn't the mode in which He spoke but how it was received by the hearer. The voice of God is not limited or confined. He speaks so that we will understand Him on a personal level.

As we come to understand the modes in which God speaks, we must also learn to recognize how we individually interpret what He is saying. My aim in this chapter is less about focusing on the many modes of revelation and more on exploring how we uniquely process that revelation.

This is what I call *prophetic personalities*. I've outlined five ways that I have found helpful for people to discover how they hear and receive God's voice. Remember, you don't have to be a prophet to be prophetic. We're all prophetic because we have all heard the voice of God. No one can become a Christian unless he or she has listened to the voice of God. Hearing God's word is the foundation of your spiritual DNA.

The five prophetic personalities are designed to help sharpen your ability to hear God. The descriptions of these personalities will give you insight into how God communicates specifically to you so that you can practice and increase your spiritual intelligence.

Unlocking your prophetic personality is not meant to pigeonhole you. These personalities can be mixed; they can have overlaps; one can be stronger in one season than in another. You'll see that I often identify with several of the personalities explained below. I don't want you to put rules or boundaries around this. These five personalities are simply guides or a starting point to help you discover how God speaks to you.

1. EXPRESSIVE

Expressive personalities take isolated incidences as signs in and of themselves. They view things as "obviously God" that others might not immediately recognize. As a common example, an expressive will start noticing double numbers (this is their *mode* of revelation) as they go about their day-to-day. They will immediately jump to the understanding that God is speaking to them through these numbers, long before other personality types might acknowledge that.

I remember a time when, just before our ministry went through a massive increase in staff and effectiveness, I began to see doubles all over the place—18-18, 12-12, 11-11—wherever I went. It became a bit of a joke in our house because I would pick up my phone at any given time and there would be double numbers on the screen.

Moments like these, for an expressive, indicate that God wants to speak. My response in these moments is to say, "God, I'm seeing a lot of double numbers. What does that mean for me?" What it means for me might be different from what it means for you, in accordance with God's direction and leading in each of our lives. What other ways does God speak to expressives? He might drop something in your spirit during your quiet time or throughout your day—a particular word or phrase—and then, all of a sudden, you see that word popping up all over the place. It doesn't seem to matter where you go: that word you felt a week ago is now appearing everywhere.

That's how God gets the attention of an expressive personality. He doesn't hide His message from you. If God is speaking to you, it will be obvious and not hidden.

2. CONTEMPLATIVE

Contemplative personalities look for patterns rather than isolated incidences. Unlike expressives, they will rarely follow a single sign in isolation. For me, an expressive, seeing double numbers might immediately jump out and propel me into action. But for a contemplative, it's not that simple. A contemplative might first have to spend time allowing that sign to percolate, and form patterns, in order to confirm that it is actually God and not simply a coincidence.

It's not that contemplatives ignore signs that others might pick up quickly; in fact, it's quite the opposite. They are intentional about taking everything in and asking the Lord about it. Often, this looks like journaling, praying, or sharing the sign with trusted friends.

God will speak to contemplatives through the finer details of life. If this describes you, you'll likely need to process, reprocess, and then internally process what you've seen or heard. If someone asks you what you're thinking, you'll likely be tempted to reply, "Uh, a whole lot of things."

Contemplatives generally love to gather all of the information before they reach a decision. It might take days for a contemplative to solidify the revelation that God has spoken, simply because of their internal processing of His word. This isn't disobedience or lack of faith; it's simply personality.

One of the things I find with contemplative personality types is their ability to connect the thread of God's goodness through every aspect of their life, or through its "grand narrative." Because they're processing every moment really well, they'll say, "Oh, I remember what God did then, and I now see how it's all connected to these signs I've been seeing."

People who hear God in a contemplative way often have a strong need to be connected relationally. They will have a few intense relationships that will help them process what's going on in their hearts. God will often use key, intimate relationships as the platform for His voice in that person's life. Often, contemplatives establish culture really well because connectedness is essential to them and they value everyone.

We see this personality in scripture via the apostle Paul, when God invaded his life and then he went to the desert for fourteen years to process that invasion. Because he was a contemplative, he needed to sort all the information God shared with him. God understands each personality and chooses to speak to us in ways that will allow us to hear and understand Him using our personalities to further His purposes through our partnership with Him.

3. STRATEGIC

Strategic personalities view signs in relation to how they contribute to a wider vision. They see how their modes of revelation work together, and they spend time pragmatically mapping out steps from one sign to another. When a strategic person begins seeing double numbers, they immediately filter the sign through the words of destiny that they've already been given. They think, *Okay, God, You're speaking; how is this sign going to help me reach my end goal.*

Hearing God's voice for a strategic is like playing connect-the-dots, with the end goal being their destiny or destination. They filter all further signs through this lens.

Unlike expressives, for a strategic, a sign from God is not meaningful in and of itself. The sign must be connected to a greater vision or strategy. God speaks in their first language: practicalities.

I often identify with the strategic personality type. For me, this looks like making decisions based on the leading of God, which sets me (or the person I'm prophesying over) up for success. For example, when I'm working with an organization that has a Christian ethos, my aim is to first marry the obvious trajectory of that organization together with any prophetic promises, and then define steps to see those things come to pass. I allow pragmatic decisions to follow prophetic prompting.

Strategists, or strategic prophetic personality types, often operate in wisdom. It's the wisdom that highlights the moment of favor; it contextualizes opportunity in the bigger picture of what God wants to do. Like chess players, strategic personalities wisely position the right people in the right places to accomplish the vision and manifest the blessing. They have an ability to recognize moments of favor and seize them.

4. ADVENTUROUS

Adventurers see signs as clues that they must follow, allowing the journey to unfold spontaneously as they go. They are not destination focused. Instead, they allow the journey to progress as the signs allow, and they love the spontaneity of this evolving plan. Adventurers are all about the journey and all about discovery.

When an adventurer begins noticing double numbers, they know the adventure is about to begin. They are comfortable with the mystery in their various signs from God, so rather than jumping to conclusions about the meaning, they ask the Lord to help them uncover more clues as to where He is leading them.

Adventurers are on a mission to discover. They look for maps, clues, and signposts. They thrive on gathering lots of little bits of information that will help decide where to find the treasure. If you relate to this personality, you'll understand that you're not merely looking for the destination; you're looking for the treasure in the moment. In some ways, the looking *is* the treasure. Adventurers will see things in the moment that others won't. Where others only see despair, you see hidden gems. You are attuned to the ebb and flow of the world around you, to following and leading.

Like sniffer dogs, adventurers follow a scent, not minding what's going on around them as they hone in on that one smell. When they uncover the truth they've been searching for, they celebrate—but not everyone understands what they're celebrating. For adventurers, it's the sheer thrill of discovery. God loves to use this personality to unlock adventure and suspense.

My friend Jesh has an adventurous prophetic personality. Recently, he was seeking wisdom about a big move; he wasn't sure where the Lord was leading him. As he went about his days, he began to notice vehicle license plates from his home state (he was living in a different state at the time). It seemed as if everywhere he went he noticed a strange number of cars with this plate.

Jesh loves discovery and knows that it's through hints and clues that God often speaks to him. Rather than presuming the license plates were a sign that he should literally go back home, he asked God what these clues meant. It was in the midst of this "adventure" that God spoke: "Home will follow you wherever you go."

5. MYSTICAL

Mystical personalities tend to live with ongoing inner dialogue in the heavenly realm. They see signs as opportunities for further mystical encounters and even search for signs in order to have these encounters. They require little confirming evidence because they are predisposed to view everything as pointing to supernatural realities.

A mystical personality will see double numbers (or even just a single number, for that matter) and immediately attach that to a supernatural or mystical experience with God. They collect these signs as they go about their day, constantly being reminded of their heavenly standing with God.

The mystical personality is very other-worldly; it's as though those with this personality type see more of the unseen realm than the world around them. They will often have deep, mystical interactions with Jesus. Mystical personalities seemingly "waste time" because they're just hanging out with Jesus.

If this is you, you tend to be very spiritually charged, often discerning the spiritual atmosphere and seeing what's going on behind the scenes. When walking into a room, you will immediately pick up on what's really going on around you. You are wired to another dimension that connects inwardly with everybody in this dimension.

Because I've learned to engage my physical and intuitive senses, I can often walk into a room and see who's struggling, through my minds eye or even physically. I see who's being oppressed demonically, where there are difficulties, tension, or joy. I can see these things without trying because the spirit world is open to me in a real and tangible way.

Mystical personalities also tend to be the kind of creatives who love to make something out of nothing. As spiritual conduits, God often uses mystics to disturb the norm, to lift our eyes out of what we see in the physical world and engage a little bit with the spiritual world. When you have a mystic who's understood by a strategist and vice versa, it's a powerful combination. The mystic will use these head-in-the-clouds, heavenly encounters, and the strategist will use his feet-on-the-ground earthiness, and together they'll give God's vision some legs to walk on.

HOW DOES GOD SPEAK TO YOU?

As you discover your personality type, you need to remember that God reserves the right to mess with your mind, speak to you in new ways, and even acknowledge an aspect of your personality that you have kept hidden or pushed down. He wants to harness your personality. When you're going about your day and doing what you usually do, He wants you to hear His voice in those everyday moments.

I'll give you an example. When I minister to executives, prior to the meeting, I'll ask Jesus what He's blessing in that person's life or business. I walk into my meetings knowing where the blessing is, and I target that. I cultivate it. I steward the information. That opens the door to greater revelation. But I've got to start somewhere, and so I start with who I am. That's the fertile ground in which God plants the word of what He wants to do in the lives of those around me.

Other times, I will walk into a room and see God highlight someone; it looks like a haze of light in a diagonal slant coming down over their head. I remember the first time that happened; I leaned over to my friend and asked if he saw the light. My friend didn't see what I was seeing. That became an indicator for me, and I understood that God was specifically speaking to me in a way I would hear Him. Now I know that when I see this light over someone, God wants to minister to that person. So, I'll go to that person and prophesy. I don't need any other reference points for what I'm about to prophesy, only that shaft of light. It's in those moments of stepping into what's natural to me that God's voice supernaturally breaks in.

It is essential that all of the personalities fit together to bring the mind of Christ to us as a people. We need one another in the unique ways we hear from God. You may feel like you relate to several of these personalities, or perhaps you once heard God as an expressive, but now you relate more closely to a mystical personality. That's okay. I find that I am more of a hybrid: I'm expressive and mystical, but I tend to carry strategy, too. I can walk into a church context, for example, where there are difficult leadership challenges, and God will give me the one line that succinctly brings the strategy that space needs in order to step into the next season. It's not because I'm trying, but because my personality carries a sense of strategy, and God speaks to me through strategy.

We often expect God to speak outside of who we are when, as it turns out, He likes His creation. For me, that is very encouraging. But it also means your spiritual journey doesn't need to look like mine. The *method* of revelation and the level of revelation aren't necessarily equal or even in competition. So, when I say I've seen an angel, and you say, "I was working out a flowchart when suddenly this idea popped into my head," your idea is as spiritually valid as my angelic encounter. This is especially true if you take what God popped into your head seriously, while I'm more caught up with the fact that my message came through an angel than I am on implementing the message itself.

We often put grades on the packaging of revelation when the point is the revelation. That moment when you're daydreaming and imagining what your business could look like, or what a particular partner needs to understand in order for your company to go to the next level—that's holy to God, and He wants to weave His thoughts in through your personality and your daily life. You don't have to over-spiritualize what you're hearing from God.

I consulted for a large company in the city of Durban, South Africa. There were unsaved people in the room who didn't have a context for prophecy or hearing from God. As I spoke, the sense of awe that filled the room was outrageous as people who knew one another felt compelled to ask, "How does this guy know this stuff?" And I wasn't shaking; I wasn't having any revival manifestations; I wasn't even talking about the angels that I was seeing in the room. I was simply communicating, very clearly and calmly, what God thought about them—His ideal possible futures for them. This created an atmosphere in which the kingdom could come. The returns for that company have been incredible.

When you discover your personality, your prophetic flow and spiritual intelligence are applied naturally. He wants to use who you are to release His purpose and His power so that His kingdom begins to transform your workplace, your place of influence, and your family to look a little bit more like heaven.

08

Favor vs. Labor

"Joseph's master took him and put him into the prison; the place where the kings' prisoners were confined, and he was there in prison. But the Lord was with Joseph, and showed him steadfast love, and gave him favor in the sights of the keeper of the prison. And the keeper of the prison put Joseph in charge of all the prisoners who were with him in prison. Whatever was done there, he was the one who did it."

Genesis 39:20-22

I want to talk about a principle that, in our work-driven society, we have forgotten: God can do more in a moment of favor than you could ever do in a lifetime of labor. Favor is a moment of destiny made available so that you can step into the incredible purposes and influence God intends for you. People like Joseph get into places of incredible favor because when God orchestrates moments, they are willing recipients and participants with God's sovereignty.

I've encouraged you to unleash the prophetic from sacred places into the public spaces. God wants you to hear His voice for your destiny and for those around you in areas that would be considered secular or unholy. He wants to restore this concept of favor in our understanding because when we grasp it, faith is activated for the impossible to happen in our circumstance.

Early in this book, we discussed what it means to live in an Eden paradigm. In Eden, everything necessary for production, fruitfulness, and life was readily available. Adam didn't have to toil to get any fruit or to sow seeds; his work was the act of stewarding what God had already put in the Garden.

The same is true for us today in the New Covenant. When you understand that His provision is already available, you'll see God provide for you and open doors for you. He wants to create a future, with your participation, that looks like His best for your life.

YOU ARE HIGHLY FAVORED

I love the story of Joseph. To me, he is one of the most incredible heroes in the Bible. God took a young man who experienced many difficult seasons of life, and right when he thought it was at the worst possible season, he found favor.

I wonder if many of us could live through such experiences, imprisoned and expecting favor to break out. Joseph was, in the Old Testament, a type and a shadow of Jesus in the New Testament: both grew in favor. Did you know that Jesus is God's favorite? He never needed to earn God's favor. He had access to that favor from the moment He was born. He did, however, grow in God's favor. As He grew in favor with God, He grew in favor with man.

I've often tried to figure out how the Son of God, the highly favored One, grows in favor. While it's clear that the measure of God's favor toward Jesus never changed from eternity past to eternity future—God wasn't saying, "I'm going to withhold some favor and give it to You in installments"—Jesus still had to grow in His reception of that favor so that He could walk in it.

Many of us don't think we have God's favor on our lives. But we each have as much favor as Jesus did. The only difference is, Jesus developed skills and spiritual intelligence, which helped Him receive that favor. The primary reason He understood how to receive favor was because of how rooted He was in His identity as God's Beloved.

Similarly, despite his situation, Joseph lived with an understanding that he was highly favored. From the moment Joseph was born, Jacob made a point of telling everyone, "This is my favorite." When you grow up with a mentality of favor, you'll see favor wherever you find yourself. But many of us have been taught to deny ourselves, to squash who we are. In doing so, we don't understand who and whose we are, and therefore we cannot walk in the great favor that God has for us. Our job is to grasp this principle of identity, believing that God has made each of us the object of His outrageous favor. Joseph understood this, and he even had a robe to remind him of it wherever he went.

FAVOR AND IDENTITY

I find it very interesting that Joseph's older brothers were jealous of him. If you don't understand your own identity, and you see favor break out on someone else, it often sparks jealousy in your heart. "Why did they get that when I didn't?" When you study older brothers in the Old Testament, you'll see this jealousy play out over and over again. You'll always see older brothers working to squash dreams instead of interpret dreams. You'll see older brothers trying to restrain passion rather than release passion. That is, until you get to Jesus.

In Luke, Jesus tells this incredible story of what really should be called "The Prodigal Father." The word "prodigal" means "lavish," and the only lavish person in Luke 15 is the father. He shares the story of one son who squanders an inheritance and the other one who never knows how to enjoy his inheritance. And the irony is that, unlike the jealous older brother in the story, Jesus is our perfect older brother. He is not ashamed to call you His brother or make you a co-heir, a co-participant, in His favor. "Both the One who makes people holy and those who are made holy are of the same family. So, Jesus is not ashamed to call them brothers and sisters."[1] That kind of favor is outrageous and unstoppable.

One of the instances that made me realize there was a deficit in my identity around the principle of God's favor was the first time I got upgraded to fly business class. It was terrific. I remember walking in there and thinking to myself, *Oh my gosh, everyone else will have to walk past me into economy class, and here I am, sitting down.* It was beautiful. And I thought I had it made, until a twelve-year-old kid walked in and took his seat across from me. He apparently came from good stock and a wealthy family, because he looked entirely at home in business class.

I, in the meantime, was fascinated by the huge screen in that section of the plane. I kept thinking, *This is going to be the best movie experience I've ever had on an airplane.* I was also fascinated by the fact that I'd be able to lie flat, which is just an amazing option when you travel as often as I do.

But this twelve-year-old was super arrogant. He walked right in, clicked his fingers at the air host, and said, "Can I please have a 7-Up? I want Smarties . . ." and he just rattled off a whole lot of stuff that he wanted. He was used to getting what he wanted because he was accustomed to business class and a lifestyle of wealth.

As I was thinking of the serious attitude adjustment he needed, I felt God say, "Son, I want you to watch him, because I want to teach you something." I watched the punk—kid, I mean kid—and realized this was old news to him. His expectation was a lot higher and more far-reaching than mine was. I was just grateful to have a seat that wasn't in cattle class, and a semi-decent steak as a bonus. But I was starting to understand what God was trying to tell me. This guy was expecting a whole lot more because he was accustomed to a level of comfort and wealth that I was not.

God then said, "Son, I want to expose a poverty spirit and a poverty mindset that's in you." I knew He wasn't wanting me to be arrogant like this boy but causing me to realize that when we understand that we are highly favored, our expectation levels are much higher. We don't live with the mindset that "I just want my needs met" or "If only we can just cover the bills this month." We live with an expectation that because we're highly favored, we can order 7-Up, the best glass of champagne, and the most expensive meal.

I felt generous Papa God say to me, "You need to understand that I own everything, and you are an heir to everything." Rediscovering that I'm a King's kid has altogether changed my expectation of favor. And please hear me: I'm not talking about living in excess or prosperity for its own sake. What I am saying, though, is that the level of expectation of favor within the body of Christ has been way too low.

God wants us to live in an ever-increasing expectation of His favor on our lives. When we get favor, we'll begin to understand that "The earth is the Lord's and the fullness thereof,"[2] and that He has given that fullness to us. In the language of business, this means that in any given context, *you* are the majority stakeholder, and your favor is not dependent on worldly position.

Joseph's understanding of favor got him promoted from the jail to one of the highest positions in the land: beside Pharaoh. God has not made us to be paupers but to be kings and queens. I have learned to assume that God's favor is going to be upon me, that more often than not, I will get what I need, in any context, because God is on my side. I happen to be His son.

FAVOR EXPANDS THE KINGDOM

One aspect of walking in favor was to learn that the favor I receive is not for my benefit but for the benefit of those around me. When

I walk in favor, I invite other people into it, as well. When you grasp something of that reality, you begin to realize that your favor-filled platform is not for you; it is a platform for anyone you influence, anyone you come into contact with. That's how favor is manifested on your life. When you understand that favor is for the benefit of others, you'll begin to realize that stewarding your favor becomes an opportunity for the kingdom of God to be extended.

I love that Joseph was willing, in the middle of a prison sentence, to interpret the other prisoners' dreams while his dream had not yet been fulfilled. He didn't complain, saying, "I haven't got my way." He realized, "I'm in charge of this prison and have a gift I can offer these two men who do not understand their dreams. Favor on me works for the benefit of those around me."

I was born in the Cape Flats—a region of Cape Town known as "apartheid's dumping ground." The Flats is where the non-white population of Cape Town were forced to establish home in an era when segregation and racial discrimination dominated the country. It's mostly residential, consisting of townships and government housing—a far cry from the rich urban areas and suburbs of Cape Town. I wasn't afforded the opportunities that many of you reading this have likely experienced. I didn't have an excellent education; my primary school had fifty students in a single classroom. You don't learn very well under those circumstances.

We were relatively poor at home. I say "relatively poor" because there were a lot of other people far worse off than we were. Our overall context, our way of life began with a deficit. We were not positioned for growth or for stepping into our destinies. I often remember interacting with white people at church (we were one of the very few people of color in our white church), feeling subservient to them because of their wealth, their well-spoken demeanor, and my skin color. I intrinsically knew I was at a disadvantage to them.

I'm so grateful for parents, however, who understood the kingdom. They knew the importance of their role in our lives and weren't focused on building a life for themselves, to meet a need; they were making a way for the next generation. I remember as a kid, standing and praying with my mum and dad, and my mum would quote, "You are the head and not the tail"[3]; "Every piece of ground that you walk on, the Lord has given unto you"[4]; "He's not given you the spirit of fear but of love, power and a sound mind"[5]; "You are more than a conqueror, through Christ Jesus who strengthens you"[6]; "Greater is He who is in you than He who is in the world."[7] The identity that she was pouring into me was not consistent with my circumstances but with who God says I am.

This provided a platform for me to wonder, *Can I do the impossible?* Growing up back in those days, the idea of travel, of going to different nations, was absolutely impossible. I couldn't even afford to get a passport, let alone a plane ticket. But at the age of twelve or thirteen, this lovely Scottish lady (Aunty Fay, of course) came to me and said, "The Lord has told me you will travel. I'm giving you your passport."

Throughout these experiences, the Lord was building my identity. Favor-filled opportunities were being stirred inside of me and I began to expect something of heaven. Now, years later, I travel into some of the most professional and intellectual contexts. I've lectured in some of the most influential schools, universities, and creative settings—not because I have a skill set to do so, but because favor can get you into places that you will never gain access to through hard work alone.

Your life is an invitation to experience favor, if you would dare believe God for the impossible. I often tell people that God changed the whole apartheid regime in South Africa so that I could travel and touch the nations, because I'm that important. I *am* that important to Him! Some might be thinking, *What an arrogant guy!* But I'm not being arrogant. I genuinely believe I'm so important to God that He was willing to shift a nation for me (and for millions of others as well).

Learning to walk in God's favor was a process, however. I realized I wasn't walking in the kind of favor or identity God had for me when I couldn't celebrate the success of others around me. I would try to make sense of others' successes: "Why did they get that deal? He probably chatted with this person, or he is an excellent networker." I'd try to dissect why someone experienced favor and I didn't. There was a deficit in my heart, and I needed to change my thought process toward favor. The reality is, God wants to release and increase your favor so that you can, without agenda and without any goal, merely extend the kingdom of His love wherever you are.

This entails moving away from "sales-pitch" evangelism to "love-based" evangelism. People can sense a sales pitch from a mile away, long before you even open your mouth. But when love is the motivation, everything changes. Once, I had the opportunity to prophesy over a corporate director in Singapore. I was sitting in this phenomenal office, thinking I would get some fantastic words about his destiny, about his future. Instead, God spoke to me about his family, his marriage, his kids, the secrets of his heart that he hadn't told anyone, and about his childhood, which he hadn't processed well. What he encountered was not destiny but love. That was the key to his future.

FILLING ALL IN ALL

The kind of favor God wants to release on the body of Christ might not ever look like more prominent church buildings, larger sanctuaries, or well-attended programs. Instead, it will be about kingdom exploits. I believe God wants to raise up billionaires who buy whole hospital chains and release free medical services to thousands of people. I believe God wants to raise up men and women who think about what it could look like to take a rundown, war-torn city and make it beautiful again. I believe for men and women who are so creative in film and industry that they're not about making dated Christian movies but shaping the imagination of a generation, as C. S. Lewis did.

This kind of favor is not merely about giving money to the church for more projects; it's about a kingdom of people who fill all in all and responsibly steward everything God gives to them. Remember Ephesians 1:22-23? God has placed everything under the feet of Jesus, and He's given it to the body to fill all in all. That means we are the primary way that heaven fills everything in the cosmos.

We need men and women who will begin to dream about a favor as profound as described in Ephesians. This level of favor is not about getting more money so you can buy a more beautiful house or a better car; it's about getting a vision of what it could look like to change a nation in a day. It's about musicians and artists who release an atmosphere of hope and love over a generation, leading them to consider their spirituality again.

It's about business people who walk into favor-filled places that they could never have worked for, to command the attention of high-level CEOs so that their hearts will be changed and the poor and marginalized—those who have been oppressed by corporate greed—come into a place of radical freedom. We don't need more capitalists who just make money, but people who make money with an understanding of the kingdom.

We won't see a renaissance, we won't see reformation in the world today, unless we get the church out of the building and into the places only favor can take us. When you understand that the measure of God's outrageous, effervescent, and overflowing favor is without end and never in question, you'll see that all He's looking for are conduits who steward that favor.

Living like that will get you out of bed in the morning as you realize that you are a walking encounter with favor for the world around you.

---

1. Hebrews 2:11
2. Psalm 24:1
3. Deuteronomy 28:13
4. Joshua 1:3
5. 2 Timothy 1:7
6. Romans 8:37
7. 1 John 4:4

09

Stewarding Favor

"(...) and whatever he did, the Lord made it succeed."

Genesis 39:23 (b)

The kingdom is not striving-oriented but stewardship-oriented. In the face of difficult situations, many of us posture ourselves for battle rather than understanding that we already have the victory. Our position should be from victory toward even more magnificent victory.

If you understand this, particularly when pursuing deals, relationships, breakthroughs, or even when you're asking God for something, you no longer approach your situation from a place of lack. Remember, just as God provided everything Adam and Eve needed in the Garden, we too have access, through Jesus, to provision and abundance. Stewarding favor is not about what you're trying to get, but rather unlocking what you already have.

Perhaps you remember the story of the talents, the two servants who grew their master's wealth and the one who hid it out of fear that he would lose it.[1] The thing is, that story has nothing to do with how hard each of the servants worked; it has to do with how they stewarded what they were given.

You are highly favored. It's who you are, not something that you have to work for or earn. You're highly favored because you're seated in Christ. Stewardship is enjoying what God has already given you. The results are up to Him. This takes all the pressure off.

STEWARDSHIP BEARS FRUIT

The temptation we experience—much like the servant in the parable—is either to try to make things happen on our own or to hide in fear that we aren't capable of using the gift or favor we've been given. For example, many people don't step into the creativity that God has called them to because they fear what other people might say about their creative expression. In this situation, stewardship looks like understanding that God has called you to be creative; all you need to do is be faithful with what He's given, and the rest is up to Him.

I had an encounter with God a few years ago, before I wrote my first book. I'd had many prophetic words—far too many to even record—that I would write a book about prophecy. I remember saying, "God, I don't have the skill set. I don't have what it takes to write this book. I don't have the know-how. I don't even know where to start. It's tough for me to even think about writing."

Not long after, I had an encounter in a meeting where there was an impartation for creativity. I knew I needed to do some writing. God spoke to me in the midst of that and said, "I've not called you to worry about how many books you're going to sell; I've called you to be faithful with what I've given you, so write the book." You see, you can have many encounters with God, but until you're faithful with that encounter—until you steward your favor—you're not going to see the manifestation and fruit.

Now, I don't have a best seller, but I was faithful with what God had given me, and I stewarded what was in my hand. The incredible thing is, I'm sitting in places of influence today that, when I wrote that book, I never could have imagined. And it's not because of the book; it's because I stewarded what God had given me. When you are faithful with little, He makes you faithful with much.

HOW TO IDENTIFY YOUR GARDEN OF INFLUENCE

There are some keys that I think might help you to grow your reception and stewardship of favor and to understand what God has called you to do. I have found the following points help me discover my role and place of influence in transforming the world.

Discover Your Tribe

You need to identify the people God has given you. The world is desperate for community, and, most often, those to whom you're connected provide the key and the breakthrough to your destiny. It is essential that you find your tribe. I'm not saying you must find people who agree with your every opinion, but who agree with heaven to see God's purposes fulfilled on the earth.

Job 22:21 says, "Agree with God, and be at peace; thereby good will come to you." The word for "agree with" means "to be acquainted with" or "to know intimately." This reveals that agreement must be understood in the context of relationship. It is not a result of demand, nor is it merely functional; but our agreement with heaven and its purposes flow out of our relationship with the Father.

While the context of this verse was the speaker condemning Job, we see the principle of agreement found throughout scripture. When we agree with heaven, the fruit that flows is pleasing. Paul tells us in 2 Corinthians 1:20 that "All the promises of God find their yes in Him. That is why it is through Him that we utter our Amen to God for His glory." Our relationship with Him is the basis from which we see His kingdom manifested. Jesus said, "If two of you agree on earth about anything you ask, it will be done for you by My Father in heaven."[2] The word "agreement" is the Greek word *sumphóneó*, from which we get the word "symphony"—the harmonizing of many voices, or many different sounds coming together to make one clear sound.

Agreement is not just about saying yes; it is the harmonious joining of hearts.

We get to choose with whom we harmonize. Find people with whom you have a deep heart connection, because those people create spheres of influence that you get to impact and be a part of. For us to change an atmosphere and see heaven's perspective released, we will have to learn how to harmonize with heaven and with one another.

I'm not simply talking about attending church or finding a good Christian community, although those are both good. I'm talking about the principle of honor that happens because of connected re-lationships. When you understand that every single person you come into contact with has value because of the intrinsic worth that the Father sets on them, you'll see they're not just your platform or your stepping stones to greatness. They become a relational partner in the journey God has called you on toward your destiny.

You need to find your tribe. You need to find your people. You need to find the people who carry something of the value system of heaven. When you do, you amplify the convergence of heaven and Earth and propel the body into its purpose and destiny.

Embrace Your Space

Part of understanding your place of influence is embracing the place where you find yourself. You are not here by accident. God has or-chestrated your life's events. Yet, God's sovereignty is not a controlling mechanism up in heaven. Remember my friend who felt trapped by the will of God? He told me, "God prophesied all these things and I don't know what to do, and I don't know where to go. If I make a wrong move, am I going to be out of His will?"

One of the greatest lies the enemy could bring to you is to convince you that God is controlling. God is not controlling. He doesn't want to control you. He wants to bring you into outrageous freedom. And because He wants to bring you into outrageous freedom, He's given you the ability to make good choices.

When people say to me that every single event that happens on planet Earth is because God wills it, I get frustrated because it's a misrepresentation of His goodness. God is secure in His sovereignty. God is so assured of His Lordship over the earth that He gives you a free choice, and He chooses to partner with your decision. This opens up an incredible vista of opportunities because God wants to invite you to dream with Him. He wants to encourage you to say, "God, I want to do this," and He goes, "Yeah, that's cool. I'll bless that." You do not have to wait for orders from heaven to fulfill your destiny. If you are, you're in slavery.

The prophetic is not meant to be a directive that binds you but a window into destiny and freedom. When you begin to understand that the choices you've made have brought you to a particular place, a context, a geography, a specific city, and a job, then you get to redeem that space as the garden of God's grace and goodness. It's where Eden begins to grow.

Your place is not an accidental spot where you happen to find yourself. It's the current culmination of your life's history. It's the flow God has brought about, intertwining with your choices, to bring you into this space that He has given you authority for.

Notice I didn't say authority *over*. Often, we think authority is about having power over another. When Jesus talks about authority to the Centurion, He makes a connection between authority, submission, and faith. The Centurion tells Him, "I am a man under authority. I say to one, 'Go,' and he goes; and to the other, 'Come,' and he comes." Jesus then says of the Centurion, "I have not seen such great faith."

Authority is not about who you are over but about who you are submitted to, and your faith in managing and stewarding the task you've been given and embracing your current space. God has given you authority for your workplace, your business, and your family, and that authority is connected to submission to Him and His goodness. The act of faith, in submitting to Him, gives you authority for the benefit of those around you.

This is an important principle in the kingdom. Jesus told His disciples to not be like the rulers of the Gentiles who "lord it over them."[3] We don't want to be those who carry our authority over someone. The real power of God is displayed not in lording it over people or trying to control them but in laying power down for something more significant: love.

The only authority that is over you is Jesus. Everything else is mutual submission, because of the grace that God has put in each one of us. The boundaries that God gave you, your space—including your house, your job, and the situations you face—were so that the authority of heaven would be expressed for the benefit of those around you.

Dare to Dream

God's primary means of accomplishing His will is through the desires of your heart. God is not wanting to conform you in such a way as to crush your personality. Rather, He wants to release you to unlock your dreams.

If you're passionate about particular things, it's because He wants to work with that. Passion is not frivolity. It's not just some whimsical thing. God wants to take the wiring that He has uniquely placed in your spiritual DNA and unlock it so that it becomes a passionate, burning force, and you live in the fullest expression of who He created you to be.

God is not a killjoy. He's not saying, "I know you really want to do that, but you're not going to. Bummer for you." He wants to unlock your passion. Passion is the essential spark that makes you come alive and it's what God put in you to bring life to you. It is within us for the sake of adventure and influence, and God wants to help you identify and walk in your passion. If it's creativity, if it's business, if it's numbers—I mean, I don't understand who could have a love for numbers, but there it is—God wants to unlock it and increase it! When I discovered this, it liberated me from the lie that I am somehow bound to the will of God in a forced way. The truth is, I get to make a choice about where I live, where I go, what I'm doing, because God partners with me and my desires to lead me into the space of His glory.

Am I looking for His fingerprints and leading? You bet I am. Am I asking Him for insight and wisdom? You bet, because He's the one whom I love. But He's not going, "If you don't do this, I'm going to smite you." So, be free to dream. What's the impossible thing that you want to do? Because God wants to meet you in the place of your passion. It is through your passion that He will reveal your garden of influence.

Look for the Moment

There are times in the life of a believer when God breaks in with a *kairos* moment. There are two words for "time" in the Bible. There's the word *chronos*, which is measured time—so, we go from one o'clock to two o'clock to three o'clock. This type of time can also be measured by seasons—summer, winter, spring. *Chronos* is quantitative; it is time measured in sequence.

The second word for time is *kairos*. In Ephesians, it talks about being careful to redeem the time. The word used there is *kairos*, which refers to an opportune time—a suitable or favorable moment. There will be times in your life when you recognize *kairos*.

I want to encourage you to be expectant for *kairos* moments. In your networking meeting, for instance, when you meet one person and think, *I really need to connect with that person*, lean into that moment, because that could be a *kairos* moment. Learn to understand the moments of God.

Growing in Influence

There will be times when it seems like God has converged many circumstances, moments, and people for your benefit and for you to release kingdom influence. If you can recognize it and grab hold of it, you will see the favor on your life multiply dramatically.

Stewardship is essential to growing in influence. In his letters to the Corinthians, apostle Paul writes about his "sphere" or "measure" of influence. He describes it as a line of influence that everyone has. And that line of influence, Paul says, is a connected relationship line.[4] In other words, where you find yourself connected to people, you share a level of influence with them. God wants to use the favor that is on your life to enhance that influence. When you understand how your favor—the gifts you've been given—impacts your level of influence, you'll steward it better.

Many of us want to increase our sphere of influence, but we've not managed to steward the area of our heart first. When we steward our heart—remember the importance of maintaining a soft, receptive heart?—we become better stewards of the relationships around us and the things God has given us. If I cannot steward my sphere of influence as it relates to my family, marriage, connections, and friendships, then I will not have authority to steward the sphere of influence in my business or in the other spaces that God might give me.

Often, the difference between a fulfilled prophetic word and a word that hasn't yet come to pass is this principle of stewardship. If you can steward well what God has given you, you'll see an increase in outrageous favor.

If you can understand your place in the grand narrative of God's story on the earth, you will know that your significance is not connected to your performance. Your importance is not related to what other people say.

Your significance is connected to your worth in His plan and in His purposes for your life. It's a beautiful thing when you realize that, despite what you need to see as "fruitfulness," you have worth in His eyes. Toward the end of Joseph's story, when he was about to reveal himself to his brothers, he told them, "Don't worry, I'm not going to smite you. I'm not going to kill you. Because you did not send me here. God sent me ahead to save a remnant, to save a nation." Joseph understood that his God-given place of favor and sphere of influence were not connected to his ability or justification for the ways he had been wronged. Joseph could've said, "I told you so; bow before me," because that's what eventually happened—his brothers bowed before him.

Instead, he acknowledged that everything was part of a bigger purpose. He understood that his personal favor, call, and destiny were connected to God's big picture on planet Earth. And the big picture is the same picture that He started with—He wants to cover the earth with a garden of delight. He wants to cover the earth with heaven, and we get the privilege of partnering with Him in accomplishing that.

---

1. Matthew 25:14-30
2. Matthew 18:19
3. Mark 10:42
4. 2 Corinthians 10:15

10
Re-creating Your World

"His divine power has granted to us all things that pertain to life and godliness, through the knowledge of him who called us to his own glory and excellence, by which he has granted to us his precious and very great promises, so that through them you may become partakers of the divine nature, having escaped from the corruption that is in the world because of sinful desire."

2 Peter 1:3-4

You get to reveal heaven's culture wherever you go. The degree to which you are aware of heaven is the degree to which you will reflect heaven. My inward value system, the way I understand heaven and the goodness of God, means that wherever I go (unless you get me on a really bad day when I've not had enough coffee), people will walk away from an encounter with me feeling more loved and seen than the moments prior to meeting me. I don't say that proudly; I say that because I know that is the culture I carry. It is the culture of heaven.

If I can honor people, love people, encourage people, then heaven breaks out in their lives. If you want to understand how to steward your favor, you have to learn to express the inward culture of your heart to everyone around you so that they come into your culture and not the other way around.

Unfortunately, much of the world has only had negative experiences with Christians, especially in the realm of business. Christians have been associated with a lack of integrity in work spaces, and we can often be vocal about what we are against rather than what we are for. Imagine if, instead, the highest level of integrity, the highest level of service, the highest level of creativity, the highest level of excellence, came from a band of people who were releasing the culture of heaven wherever they went.

One of the things that I've had to learn how to do is release the culture of heaven impartially to people who I disagree with. I have been in a position where I've been asked to prophesy over people who might have a different political view, or who might even be oppressors. I have an opportunity to either release heaven's culture or my opinion to them. Those are two vastly different experiences for that person. One releases freedom (the culture of heaven) and the other releases my own agenda.

The reason why many Christians don't have a clearer voice in government is that their agenda is a political agenda rather than a kingdom agenda. The same can be said of business, entertainment, and media. Are we releasing the culture of heaven in our sphere of influence or the culture of our own opinion and agenda? There is nothing quite so impactful as people who can serve, even in an oppressive regime, to bring about the kingdom. Joseph, Daniel, Moses, Jesus, and Paul all had to do exactly that.

When you live in the dynamic of creating the atmosphere and culture over your area of influence, everything changes. Those around you suddenly say, "Why is it I feel loved even when we disagree?" "Why is it that I feel like you really value my opinion, even when I'm not the key player in this deal?" It's because you're releasing a culture that looks and feels different from what they are used to.

The real call for Christians is that we become the cultural architects of our cities, of our workplaces, and of our spheres of influence. When people walk into your space, they should say, "This is a different culture. What is it?"

Imagine businesses where the aim is not competition but provision. It's not about who gets the first prize but about who gets to share in the ultimate prize. That's what heaven looks like. The goal of the kingdom isn't capitalism or more money or more things. It's not about the "early bird" like we so often tell ourselves. In the kingdom, there's more than enough for everyone. The goal of the kingdom is releasing heaven, provision, and resources so that the very least in the kingdom are lifted up.

"RE-CULTURIZING" YOUR SPHERE OF INFLUENCE

In the previous chapter we looked at ways to identify your sphere of influence, whether it is the space you find yourself in, your community, your workplace, or a new opportunity made available in a *kairos* moment.

But what does it look like, practically, to bring the culture of heaven to your realm of influence? What does it look like to "re-culturize" and re-create our world?

These are several key areas that are significant issues in our world today and where our world is crying out for change, wisdom, and understanding.

POLITICS

The Bible tells us that the kingdoms of this world will become, and are becoming, the kingdoms of our God. But what does that mean? Any worldly system—whether it be communism, socialism, democracy—is nothing compared to what the kingdom looks like.

The kingdom is led by an incredible King called Jesus who models His kingship not by grasping for power or position, not by legislating a Christian worldview, not by trying to get people into uniformity or systems that make them do what He wants them to do.

That kingdom led by our King looks like a life laid down. It looks like letting go of power, letting go of position, in order to demonstrate a new way of love. A new way of being human—that's what Jesus modeled for us.

The hope of our nation is not in getting the right government in place, and it's not in getting the right president in place. In fact, I don't believe the kingdom is designed to function as Christian countries that legislate Christianity. Rather, I believe that the kingdom always works in obscurity.

Jesus talks about the kingdom being like a mustard seed; it drops into nothing, but it begins to grow and demonstrate God's kindness. The way the kingdom grows is not through finding positions of power; it's not through voting for the "right" people. I do believe it is important to vote. I lived in a country where I couldn't vote for many years. I believe in voting wisely, and I believe in voting for what looks like kingdom values on display.

But I will not find hope in a politician or a "king" in this world. I only find hope in a King called Jesus. The hope of seeing the kingdom demonstrated is not through legislating laws that protect our freedom (although that's important); it's through demonstrating lives that look like the kingdom.

The kingdom looks like laying down our lives for others, loving the one in front of us, lifting the poor and the broken. It looks like bringing an end to human trafficking, making sure that we stop modern-day slavery, and making sure that we engage with the issues around us through a kingdom lens of love. It looks like freedom and security for *everyone*. In the kingdom, we treat the immigrant with love. We also don't try to self-protect, because, ultimately, God is the one who protects us.

My nation, South Africa, has seen some of the worst xenophobia, which has led to incredible violence. That's not what the kingdom looks like. The kingdom begs the question "How do I serve the one who's oppressed?" It does not look like me waiting for a politician to try to change laws. Instead, we must remember the truth: We are the expression of the King and His kingdom. We are the expression of His love and His kindness. We are the expression of *shalom*.

The Bible says that the government of Jesus is a government of peace. It is our role to make things the way God always intended them to be. We are the shoulders on which that government rests. We are the demonstration of peace to the world around us. How we live our lives is ultimately what changes culture, which changes hearts, which brings transformation, which changes a country and disciples a nation.

It is not simply about who you vote for but, rather, how you live. Are you good news to the poor? Are you good news to the broken? Are you living from a place of love? Because the only government that is being established on the earth is the government through which the church demonstrates the kingdom.

There are many principalities and powers. The word "principality" means "first ruler." The first ruler over any given area should be the church, because we are seated in heavenly places in Christ Jesus. When we demonstrate the kingdom through love and establish a government of peace on Earth, eventually it will topple every other government, and every other expression, until we begin to see the kingdom of God fully established on the earth. And there will be a day when He comes back and His government will finally cover everything and all things will be made new. Until then, we should be a prophetic picture of the kingdom through the way that we live.

RACISM

I grew up in apartheid-era South Africa for the first half of my childhood. This meant that, because of my skin color, I lived in an area that was demarcated for people of color, for non-whites. It meant that schooling sucked for me. It meant that I couldn't do the stuff that most people would consider normal, solely on the basis of my skin color. The racial division was systemic, in that the government thought out ways to suppress a whole people group, and to impact their psychology and their family make-up. Every aspect of what makes a society a functioning society was broken down and repackaged through the lens of racism.

I'm so glad that Jesus is so kind and that He modeled what it looks like to reach out to people beyond what He looked like. The way He related to women, minorities, other races, the poor, the broken, is unlike anything that was seen in His day. He was, and is, the ultimate bridge builder. He breaks through some of the worst relational tensions simply because He values love. And the way He demonstrates that is by breaking through into people's hearts.

But the reality is that the kingdom of God looks like every nation, every tribe, every tongue, and every culture demonstrating love and worship before God. Cultures represent the multifaceted nature of God, because God is more glorified in diversity than He is in uniformity. Our sonship is not to be confused with uniformity. God wants us to be unique in our culture, in our identity, and in our skin color so that we reflect who He is.

However, our culture, or our skin color, is not the ultimate expression of our identity. Our identity is primarily expressed through being sons of God. This is not a Jewish identity; I don't need to become Jewish to be a son of God. Neither is it an American or English identity. Our faith and status as children of the King is not connected to our national identity. It is simply this: you are a son of God, and being a son of God means that your identity is wrapped in the incredible kindness and grace of Jesus. That"s it. I am not just my skin color, my background, my culture, or my nationality. And neither are you.We are sons and daughters of God.

This is the kingdom lens through which we should view the world around us. And it is the reality that should impact how we re-create our world.

The Bible tells us we need to be liberal with all things. Because my people were systematically oppressed, I want to make sure that how I choose to be liberal in all things—share the stuff that I have been given—breaks some of the systems that have been built around racism and suppression. I want to help provide an opportunity for people to become all that they need to be. It means that the call to be liberal impacts both my wallet and my heart. It impacts how I love. How I release education and how I share resources—all of that is impacted by the need and desire to break the back of systemic racism.

Ultimately, though, we should be driven by love—not a liberal agenda, not even a freedom agenda, just love. In South Africa, there were a band of people called the Freedom Fighters who fought for our freedom. And as is so often demonstrated throughout history, the people who fight for freedom become oppressors in the next generation. I believe this happens because we haven't learned to transition from being freedom fighters to being freedom fathers and mothers. We haven't learned to steward that freedom and pass it on to the next generation.

I want to be one of those who fight for freedom and who also create opportunities for people of all colors to experience that freedom and be all that they were created to be. I do not want to fight for freedom, however, in a way that divorces it from love. Because, ultimately, love covers a multitude of sins. Justice in the kingdom of God looks like freedom for everyone. It looks like those who are oppressors suddenly becoming who God has called them to be so that they oppress no longer. It looks like those who have been victims of oppression suddenly becoming free and powerful and no longer victims. The ground at the foot of the cross is equal for both the oppressor and the victim. And just as Jesus demonstrated, we need to find ways that bridge our differences, the way we see and relate to one another, through love and kindness and open-hearted conversations.

The issue of racism is a heart issue, and until the human heart is changed, philosophy and political persuasion are not going to eliminate racism. You cannot legislate heart change. It has to be a work of the Spirit. And so, for me, as a person of color, I've learned to forgive white oppressors who kept my family suppressed for a long time. I've learned to build relationships with people who transcend the basis of my culture or color and connect with them on the basis of a kingdom reality, where love is the currency.

PRIVILEGE

The issue of privilege, and particularly white privilege—because most often it is that particular group that experiences privilege—is an

interesting one. The reality is that there are those who are more privileged and those who are less privileged. But what does privilege—
and equality—look like in the kingdom? What is the culture that we
need to change or adjust when it comes to privilege?

When we find ourselves in a place of privilege, the kingdom beckons
for hearts of sustainable generosity.

If we see the kingdom of God through the lens of capitalism, we fo-
cus on working hard and keeping what we earn. It's not a bad thing
to work hard; it's not a bad thing to keep what you earn and steward that wealth. However, this is not the value of the kingdom. In the
kingdom, there is more than enough for everyone, and God is the
ultimate provider—not your job, not your education, not your history, not your skin color. Money and privilege do not set you up for
success. God sets you up for success.

The reality is that God pours out grace upon everyone. God provides
for people. That is the lens of the kingdom: not to simply bring an
equal playing field for everyone, but learning to be liberal and generous with all that we have, because it all belongs to God.

We can change the culture of privilege by giving to things that actually make a difference. We can sow into the lives of people who are
doing incredible work in different parts of society that releases a sustainable increase of blessing. We can use our privilege by stewarding
hearts of generosity, making sure that we educate and uplift, and giving into spaces where we, ourselves, don't have a direct impact.

But more than that, it's about realizing that your house, your car, your
job are all given to you because God is kind. When we realize that we

don't own what we have, we begin to live a life of faith. What does that mean? When God moves upon my heart to give tens of thousands of rands or dollars away, I do that because I realize that I'm stewarding what He has given me. When you live like that, you start to see the needs of others. You start to think through the lens of "How do I equip those around me? How do I re-create my world?"

In South Africa, it is common to have a domestic helper who works in your home. Many of my friends have had a domestic helper their whole lives. Yet that domestic helper doesn't share in any inheritance, doesn't share in land, doesn't share in education. In fact, the average wage of a domestic helper is far below what would be considered a living wage. When we were still in South Africa, Katia and I made a decision to not just pay our domestic helper a salary but to pay her a living wage—not because we had the money but because we felt like that was fair. That's what the kingdom looks like.

Not only that, but we also worked hard on getting her a driver's license so that she could have better prospects for her next job. Our goal was to introduce to her a new culture, a new worldview. We wanted to help move her out of a context of simply working for below minimum wage. We wanted to bless, to give way above. We wanted to share our wealth in terms of genuine equity so that in her next season of life she could start off on a better platform—and all because God blessed us so that we could share that blessing with her.

When we start to understand our privilege and blessing in terms of a gift that can be given away, we spread the culture of heaven wherever we go. This is true with our finances but also with our homes and families. What if every Christian considered adoption? What if every child of color, every underprivileged child, had a home? Every

Christian *should* consider adoption and listen for God's heart on that issue. It's not an option. It doesn't mean that you have to adopt, but it does mean that we should all ask God, "Is adoption a way for me to help lift people up into a new place of freedom?" That is "re-culturizing" our world.

If the gospel is not good news to the poor, then it's not the gospel. And good news to the poor means lifting them up out of their poverty, out of their brokenness, out of systemic racism, out of systemic oppression, out of systems that have kept people in particular demographics oppressed for multiple generations. We have to make a difference; it's not up to politicians. The kingdom is good news. It's not about who you vote for; it's not about the policy or the party that's in power. It's about the church taking responsibility, according to the Bible, for widows and orphans, the broken and the hurting. When we do that, things change, societies change, and we become the hope of the world.

CAPITALISM

As we examined earlier, the kingdom is a system that doesn't look like the world's systems. I find it fascinating that the people of Israel wanted a king like the other nations of the world. God said to them, "I'm your King," but the people of Israel insisted, "No, no, we want a king like the world."[1]

Samuel argued and tried to convince the Israelites that God's kingdom and reign were superior to an earthly kingdom. By choosing a king to judge them, they were choosing an inferior kingdom. In this same way, the earthly systems of today—in this case, capitalism—also do not reflect the kingdom.

When I think about the kingdom as it is expressed in the Bible, I think about a kingdom that is not looking for resources that it already has. I think about a kingdom that's not trying to work hard to get anything. Instead, the Bible says that all wealth, all glory, all riches, are already God's. Which means that when I come into the kingdom, I'm not trying to earn a living. I'm not trying to work for something. I'm not trying to work for my house. I'm not trying to work for anything, because it's already being provided for me in the gracious, kind work of Jesus on the cross.

Everything that the Bible says I need for life in godliness has been given to me.[2]

From this perspective, I wonder if we have used capitalism as a cover for greed. We've made capitalism the goal and the god of our provision, when actually God is our provider. We don't have to buy into the systems of this world. It doesn't mean that working for something is irrelevant; the Bible says that work is good and godly. It doesn't mean that enjoying favor and prosperity is bad. Rather, seeing through the lens of Jesus and how He lived demands that we adjust our view of capitalism.

We need a more compassionate view of capitalism. In other words, when you see capitalism through the lens of the kingdom, what you see are systems that can be harnessed for the sake of the broken, for the hurting, and for the poor.

Instead of being power hungry, we become servant-hearted. Instead of being competitive, we become humble. Jesus never grasped at equality or power with God; He humbled Himself and served. When you see the kingdom of God and you apply that to capitalism, you realize that it's not your powerful position that counts; it's your posture of servanthood that counts.

When you see that love as the primary vehicle for why you earn money, for why you get to be prosperous, you suddenly stop making it about yourself and learn to rest in the goodness of God and allow Him to provide for you. When you live like that, it becomes an adventure, because you get to be a conduit of blessing for those around you.

We discussed kingdom generosity earlier in this book, but I want to emphasize it here again in juxtaposition to capitalism. How you spend your money reveals what you believe about God's kingdom. I don't know if you've noticed this, but heaven is not experiencing a recession. I've observed two very extreme reactions to kingdom finances and wealth. One extreme is the idea that we need to remain poor and humble because that's supposedly a virtue of heaven. The other extreme says, "The richer I am, the more it's a sign of God's blessing on my life, so if I'm not really rich, then I'm probably not really blessed." Both extremes are unbiblical. But when you understand that in the kingdom there's more than enough, it's not what you have that expresses your worth but what you give.

I cannot tell you how many people are offended by my sense of style. People will often say, "For a minister of the gospel, you dress really well!" "Oh, I see you've got another new watch. Wow, you must have a lot of money. You know, those offering baskets must be big!" What they don't know is that I give so, so much away—clothes, watches, and other stuff—that I have now hit a place of overflow. The Bible says that what you sow, you reap; I can't help but get given brand-new stuff all the time, wherever I go. It's not like I'm trying!

But because I've been generous and have shared what I already have, I understand that even when it looks like I'm going to go without, there's more than enough in the kingdom. I've given away three watches, and I've received about seven watches in return. One of them is worth 100,000 rand (around 7,000 U.S. dollars), an extravagant piece I would not have thought to purchase for myself. When you live a lifestyle of generosity with what you have, prosperity is the result.

For those of you who struggle with this principle, let me explain. In Psalm 67 it says the blessing of God will come upon His people in such an outrageous way that it will cause nations to fear God. His outrageous blessing on your life will be an opportunity for evangelism. It will be an opportunity for people to connect with God. And for those of you who think the principle of blessing only works in the affluent West—or in the context of capitalism—God's provision exists outside the bounds of nations, lifestyle, race, or any other dividing factor. I've been in the bush-bush of Africa (not to be confused with the bush, which is only rural, not *really* rural). I've seen hard places, and even in those places, provision comes in the form of supernatural activity. It might not come in the form of a million bucks, but God provides in the most unlikely ways because that is who He is: He's a supernatural provider. Our culture needs to look different, and change will happen when we become outrageous givers.

GENDER EQUALITY

The final area I want to touch on with regard to re-creating our world is this idea of gender equality. This is a topic that is both prevalent in and out of the church, an area of reform that our culture is crying out for. God spoke to me really clearly when I was eighteen that one of the roles of the prophetic is to unlock a sense of gift and call for women. I feel personally called to see women championed and released to do whatever they feel God has called them to do. It is our role as the church to demonstrate to the world heaven's perspective and God's heart for women.

In the kingdom, there are no restrictions for women. They can operate in any area of government or leadership, both in the church and outside the church. I began to discover, as I'm married to this beautiful, strong, gifted Bible teacher and leader called Katia Adams, that it is so much fun finding out what her gifts are and what my gifts are and how they fit together. From that place of understanding each other's strengths and weaknesses, we can allow each other to lead based on our specific areas of strength and to cover each other in our areas of weakness.

When we got married, rather than make a blanket statement about a wife submitting to her husband, we both said we will submit to each other, because the Bible, in Ephesians, calls for mutual submission. This is also how the Trinity works; they do this beautiful dance called *perichoresis*. In the moment, for example, the Father is needed, He seems to rise and reveal Himself as the Father. But then, as we see in Galatians, the Bible says, "But when the fullness of time had come, God sent forth his Son."[3] And so we see Jesus coming at the right time and He's shining. And then we see Jesus ascending, and the Holy Spirit is poured out. The Trinity does this dance around one another so that at any given moment they fully represent each other, but they also give each other space to take the limelight.

That is what Katia and I are doing with each other, and I think that's how it should work in the body of Christ. The Bible (particularly in the book of Corinthians) emphasizes the importance of the grace gift that God has given a particular person, irrespective of their gender, and the moment God is calling them to shine.

Re-creating our world in the area of gender equality is about submission; kingdom relationships look like submission. That's what Paul calls us to in the book of Ephesians. What we need in the body of Christ is for women not just to have a platform but also to have influence—real influence—with authority, because God has called us to be equal and to carry the same authority. That's what it means to be a son or a daughter of God. No ceilings. No restrictions. No "You can do this, but you can't do that."

I am so excited about what God is doing on the earth today in liberating women to not only find their voice but also to find their unique, God-gifted authority for the purpose of coming alongside men, as we mutually submit to one another. Together, we can be released into the destiny that God has for us and see the kingdom of God come in every sphere of life, in every way possible, through every person. That is heaven on Earth. That is what it means to "re-culturize" our world.

---

1. 1 Samuel 8 (paraphrase)
2. 2 Peter 1:3
3. Galatians 4:4

11
Love Is Authority

"You cannot have authority over that which you do not love."

Shawn Bolz

While I was a youth pastor, I got to foster a fifteen-year-old boy. His family was super dysfunctional. After being abandoned by his mother at the age of three, he was reunited with her at thirteen, only to be kicked out of her house two years later.

I had never met a young man with so much anger. I remember his pent-up frustration and his dull-grey eyes full of sadness. After his first few nights of visiting our youth group, I had the opportunity to pray for him. Well, it was more like a long, ugly cry and hug than anything spiritually articulate. But for the first time, he felt loved. After that moment, his eyes turned sparkling blue (and they still are that way to this day) and his demeanor completely changed. It was beautiful.

God spoke clearly to me about having him come and live in my tiny, two-bedroom flat. As a twenty-three-year-old youth pastor, the thought of a teenager moving in with me was crazy. Love looks crazy sometimes!

From that moment on, all I did was love him. I taught him how to enjoy God and to cook. I really love cooking, so we cooked a lot. And believe it or not, that was the key to unlocking his destiny. My adopted son—well, now he is more like a brother—is married, has his own family, and is a leading chef in one of Cape Town's top restaurants. Love—and some amateur cooking skills—unlocked his destiny.

LOVE LOOKS LIKE SOMETHING[1]

Love looks like stewarding relationships. Love looks like having grace toward others. But here's the deal: your ability to love others is directly connected to the way you love yourself. The reason most Christians cannot really love people is that they don't really know how to love themselves. You're not a sinner; you're not evil; you're not a failure; you're not pathetic. Those words—and identities—are unacceptable for a Christian. You're a saint! You're highly valued, beloved, and you have a place of purpose in God's family.

If you do not believe that about yourself, you'll never come into your destiny. At some stage, you're going to have to believe what Jesus says about you—that your sins are forgiven. At some stage you're going to have to believe that when Jesus died, naked on the cross, He wanted to remove the shame and guilt that are connected to the memory of your sin. He did that so you can walk freely, without shame and without hiding anything. The reality is, He knows it all anyway and He still loves you. God is not disappointed with you. He has never been disillusioned by your choices. He knows who you are; He never had any illusions about you in the first place. And He continues to love you.

If love is not the motivating factor, then this is all worthless. And loving yourself means showing grace to yourself. In the midst of failure, grace says, "I'm still loved. I'm still accepted. God still thinks I'm the bee's knees. God still thinks the best thoughts about me." It is the beauty of the gospel that God redeems your absolute worst thoughts about yourself and replaces it with His best thoughts about you.

Spiritual intelligence will be of no use to you if you don't know how to love. I want to invite you into love encounters with the Father that are possible out of the overflow of His love for you. It's a challenge when you have to love leaders who don't have integrity. It's a challenge when you have to love people who have spoken about you and sinned against you. It's a challenge!

Love does not deny wrongdoing; love chooses to overlook it. Love doesn't negate the pain that's caused by wrongdoing; love chooses to process through it and value the person, regardless of what they've done. How is your love life? How well do you love yourself? This is essential to effectively learning to love those around you and to spreading the kingdom and God's original intent to all the world.

ARTICULATING HOPE

Part of our call to redeem the earth and make all things new, part of walking in love, is being able to articulate the hope of the gospel to the world. The church hasn't done well in releasing a language and articulating the gospel in a way that makes sense to non-Christians. "Christianese," as it is often referred to, is quite a unique language, and only certain communities speak that language. Most other people think we're slightly daft when we speak in our church-based language. We need to learn how to be naturally supernatural in how we share the gospel.

I don't have to speak loudly in tongues to get my breakthrough in the boardroom; I just need to be me. One of the greatest things that the world needs in this season is a new language, the language of hope and love. Now, I've read the end of the story: we win. The ending is good, not bad. The world is not going to hell in a hand basket, I promise you. In fact, everything will be redeemed, all things will be made new and, in the words of the anchoress Julian of Norwich, "All shall be well, and all shall be well and all manner of thing shall be well."[2]

While we wait, hope is increasing. Life is increasing. More people are getting saved today than at any other time in history. The gospel is still doing what it's always done: changing the world. I can tell you story after story about people encountering God in the Middle East. I can tell you story after story about people encountering God in boardrooms in New York—because the gospel works in whatever context it's in. The Bible suggests that the only ones who get raptured from the earth are the evil ones. Jesus will establish His kingdom over everything, and all things will be made new. If you live with an eschatology that is an escapist mentality, your language will always be full of defeat and hopelessness.

We must demonstrate this hope in every area of our lives, both through supernatural displays of God's power and the everyday expressions of love. A great bumper sticker I saw recently said, "Jesus is coming soon, look busy." Let's get on with being hope dispensers in everything we do! As N. T. Wright says, "What you do in the present—by painting, preaching, singing, sewing, praying, teaching, building hospitals, digging wells, campaigning for justice, writing poems, caring for the needy, loving your neighbor as yourself—will last into God's future. These activities are not simply ways of making the present life a little less beastly, a little more bearable, until the day when we leave it behind altogether. They are part of what we may call building for God's kingdom."[3]

LOVE IS NOT WEAK

Love always points to the truth. I am not talking about truth as a concept or a philosophical ideology. I am talking about a person called Jesus. He is truth personified. How we love needs to look like Him, point to Him. On Earth, He was both unconditional in expressing love and entirely comfortable with addressing issues and cultural nuances that did not reflect His Father's kingdom.

Often, our modern-day push to political correctness calls us to unconditional approval rather than unconditional love. The truth is that not everything man does warrants approval, especially under the disguise of love. Love does not mean I approve of everything; it means I see everyone's inherent worth and choose to love that unconditionally.

As I write this, I am in the midst of some forceful engagements on social media. The conversation stems from a post that challenged the popular premise that only a Christian political party will make a difference in my home nation, South Africa. Many people I respect and love are in a place of political influence, and some of them ascribe to what they would consider a "Christian" party. While I want to show respect and love toward those I disagree with, the call to vote for "the only righteous party," and judge anyone who votes differently, is both unhelpful and goes against scripture.

A party of this type makes the statement that "We are the ones who have the truth" and all other political parties or ideologies are incorrect. The problem is, the church has largely engaged truth through the lens of reductionism. We reduce our arguments over the "issues" to one or two verses in the Bible and miss the point of incarnational living. We love to use Jesus' anger in the temple as our reasoning for a "truth in love" mentality. There was a lot more going on in the temple cleansing than Jesus getting angry with corrupt priests. The Jewish temple system excluded people from worshiping there. When Jesus came to cleanse the temple, His prophetic act was not a violence against people but against the system that built walls and separated the chosen ones and the outsiders. Jesus is not just a King for one ethnicity but for all nations. He was declaring that heaven is now accessible for every nation through prayer and not through religious systems (for a more in-depth look at this, I suggest reading N. T. Wright's "For Everyone" commentaries).

Jesus lived in the light of God's kingdom by demonstrating what it looks like to love in flesh and blood. His worldview acted as yeast, empowered by the Spirit, as He journeyed with a community of ragtag followers to change the narrative of a whole region—and the world. For us to have authentic influence, our aim as Christians cannot be world domination. I often hear teachings on the seven mountains of influence that lean toward dominion theology, which demands that all things be Christianized. In this scenario of a "Christian" political party, the government is led by Christians, and Christian principles are legislated and pasted onto existing world structures.

The problem is, as we discussed earlier, you cannot legislate heart change. The result of this kind of thinking, in its extreme, are events like the Crusades, an era when religious armies fought and forced people to become Christian. This has been tried before: "But the people refused to obey the voice of Samuel. And they said, 'No! But there shall be a king over us, that we also may be like all the nations, and that our king may judge us and go out before us and fight our battles.'"[4] It did not end well for Israel. Authority based on world systems always fails.

Like Israel, the church has often traded godly authority for worldly systems. In Matthew 20, Jesus was on His way to Jerusalem, and His disciples had still not grasped that His kingdom would not come via a coup d'état but through His life laid down as a ransom for many. His words to them were, "You know that the rulers of the Gentiles lord it over them, and their great ones exercise authority over them. It shall not be so among you. But whoever would be great among you must be your servant."[5]

The goal of influence is not control. No matter what mountain of influence you climb, what establishes real authority is not control but love—love that has no agenda and is simply there for a revelation that points to the kindness of God. As Greg Boyd rightly says:

Participants in the kingdom of the world trust the power of the sword to control behavior; participants of the kingdom of God trust the power of self-sacrificial love to transform hearts. The kingdom of the world is concerned with preserving law and order by force; the kingdom of God is concerned with establishing the rule of God through love. The kingdom of the world is centrally concerned with what people do; the kingdom of God is centrally concerned with how people are and what they can become. The kingdom of the world is characterized by judgment; the kingdom of God is characterized by outrageous, even scandalous, grace.[6]

This is the most essential part of this book: The way you grow in favor in the spheres of influence that God gives you is through the currency of love. The authority that God expresses on the earth today is not through His power; the power that God reveals on the earth today is because He is love.

We are to have the same mind as Christ. "Have this mind among yourselves, which is yours in Christ Jesus, who, though he was in the form of God, did not count equality with God a thing to be grasped, but emptied himself, by taking the form of a servant, being born in the likeness of men. And being found in human form, he humbled himself by becoming obedient to the point of death, even death on a cross."[7]

Jesus' model of spiritual revolution and cultural change is not to stay in the right "position"; it's not to grasp at authority. Instead, it is to lay down His life. Most often, the route to favor-filled influence is not the way of networking or position climbing but of love-filled servanthood.

If you do not live in love, you will not have the authority to change the things around you. The authority that gave Jesus influence was because of love. His apostolic mission flowed from love: "For God so loved the world."[8] This was His directive and the empowering dynamic of His legitimate authority.

The transient nature of love as expressed by Hollywood is weak and ineffective to change anything. The love that Jesus operated in was before time, over time, and is eternal in nature. It was in love that He adopted us even before the foundations of the earth.[9] It was this love that rose Jesus from the dead.

NO MORE TEARS AND PAIN

There will be an end to this age. It, too, will pass. While we wait for that, there will be a great harvest of souls and many will be saved in these days. We will see the kingdom come in its fullness. All things will become new—no more tears, no more pain, no more sickness, God's rule and reign fully expressed with no sin to block it.

When Paul promises us in Romans 6:23 that "The wages of sin is death, but the gift of God is eternal life," the word used for life is *zoë*, the God kind of life—full of effervescent joy and energy, which come from Him. The age to come is for us, now. We are receiving kingdom life in ever-increasing installments right now. That's how we do miracles and demonstrate the kingdom. It's all by the Spirit. The *shalom* of the kingdom is coming by the Holy Spirit.

People have said to me, "Julian, you expect too much of what God will do now." My response is this: when I have exhausted all that Jesus did in His earthly ministry, then you can accuse me of having an over-realized eschatology. Until then, the two things I often say are

"More, Lord" and "*Maranatha*, Jesus!"

We need to make our world beautiful. We need to rediscover Eden, because when we understand that Eden is within us, the garden around us will begin to look a little bit more like heaven.

I greatly desire to see you unlocked to be all you were created to be so that you become a person of influence in whatever sphere of society you operate. For that, you must believe that every aspect of your life, from your family to friendships to work to recreation, can come under heaven's influence because you have access to that realm. I want you to discover that by returning to look at Eden, by understanding God's love for you and for all of humanity, you can change the world around you to look more like heaven. The original intent of Eden is still God's intent for you today.

Go and re-create the world!

---

1. I have often heard Heidi Baker say this in her preaching.
2. Julian of Norwich, *Revelations of Divine Love*.
3. N. T. Wright, *Surprised by Hope: Rethinking Heaven, the Resurrection, and the Mission of the Church*.
4. 1 Samuel 8:19-20
5. Matthew 20:25-26
6. Gregory A. Boyd, *The Myth of a Christian Nation: How the Quest for Political Power Is Destroying the Church*, n.p.
7. Philippians 2:5-8
8. John 3:16
9. Ephesians 1:4-7

Ab

About the Author

For more information on
products and free resources,
visit www.frequentsee.org/resources.

JULIAN ADAMS

Julian is a co-director of Frequentsee. He is an author, spiritual advisor, revelatory teacher, and leadership consultant in political, business, and creative spheres. An internationally recognized prophet, Julian has a proven track record in the fulfillment of words released over individuals, communities, and nations. Julian loves cooking, jazz, playing rough-and-tumble with his kids, and date nights with his wife, Katia. Julian is also the author of *Gaining Heaven's Perspective, Amplify: Refining Your Prophetic Gift, The Kiss of the Father*, and co-author of *7 Keys to Living Big*.

MORE FROM
Julian Adams

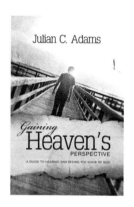

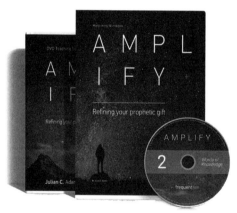

ALL FOUND AT
frequentsee.org